Snippets of Memories

DONNA KARLIN

Copyright © 2015 by Donna Karlin. All rights reserved worldwide.

ISBN: 1505240271
ISBN-13: 978-1505240276

Published in the United States

No part of this publication may be reproduced, stored in a retrieval system, or transmitted in any form or by any means, electronic, mechanical, photocopying, recording, scanning, or otherwise, except as permitted under Section 107 or 108 of the 1976 United States Copyright Act, without the prior written permission of the author.

Requests to the publisher for permission should be addressed to the Permissions Department at *A Better Perspective*© 613.829.7539 or via email at info@abetterperspective.com

Limit of Liability/Disclaimer of Warranty: While the author has used her best efforts in preparing this book, they make no representation or warranties with respect to the accuracy or completeness of the contents of this.

Donna Karlin Photo by Doug Ellis Photography. Photos within the book from family, friends and internet archives, and photographers unknown.

A Better Perspective® is a registered trademark of Donna Karlin.

ABP Publishing

FIRST EDITION

DEDICATION

To my amazing family; thank you for such indelible memories. And to you, Dad, wherever you are, as Michael would say, we know you are the life of the party.

We miss you.

CONTENTS

	Introduction	i
1	Dufferin Road	1
2	Lac Paquin	23
3	Pets and Sundry	39
4	Honey Cakes, Hot Dogs, Latkes and More	59
5	It's All About Family - Mental Snapshots	87
6	Trips to New York	99
7	Niagara Falls	111
8	Another Chance: Our Trip to Florida	115
9	Snapshots of Memories From Other Trips	121
10	Camp Hiawatha	133
11	Moving Away & Trips Back Home	141
12	Some More Random Snippets	149
	In Summary	153
	About the Author	161

Home is where our story begins...

My memories of our family are like a scrapbook of images, scents and sounds that come and go. They are triggered by the biggest or smallest of things from the smell of raspberries or freshly baked yeast dough, to the crunch of the snow under my boots, the snow-laden branches of the pines and evergreens, or the crackling sound of a roaring fire. These memories bring back mental snapshots that continue to inform, enrich and influence my life every day.

INTRODUCTION

Stories worth telling are the ones that strike closest to your heart.

When Dad was in the hospital in palliative care, I came across this mug which said it all, "Life is a story. Make yours a best seller." Dad did make his a best seller. Yes, there were difficult times and yet he could look me in the eye and say, "I have no regrets. Did I wish I did some things differently? Yes. But overall, I have had a great life and couldn't ask for anything more." That's where the conversation took place about writing some of the stories of experiences I shared within my family. This isn't a book about my career; it's about the meaning of family and how it has enriched my life exponentially.

Over the years I have written about scent-triggered memories of our time in the country, and the family values I was brought up with. Some of these memories are almost as strong today as the time they happened. To me, it's a reminder of what is so precious — the gift of the special people in our lives and time with them to create such powerful memories.

Some of these traditions are carried on in our homes today. There is often a roaring fire going. Winter time we have a jigsaw puzzle in the works on the table for anyone to try to find that specific piece or the edge 'right there'. There's still some needlework on the go, or a quilt close by so I can put in a few stitches here and there.

Just like at our home in Lac Paquin, the special people in our lives are always welcome. If there's something to serve them to eat, they help themselves and if not there's always a cup of tea or coffee, or a glass of wine and a conversation waiting to happen and the rest unfolds as it should.

The trees that surround the house remind me of those in the country and once in a while even Harvey, the six foot three and a half inch rabbit makes an appearance on TV.

Home should be welcoming and warm, a place that stays in our hearts and minds forever.

I know many would say they have the most unique family, but in many ways ours is different. We are closer than close. Our family members are our friends by choice and those friends we've had for decades are our family by choice. Even more out of the ordinary is that the subsequent generations have adopted the same perspective of family and are as close to each other as we were growing up.

This book is about just that — family; how we laugh together, cry together, rally around each other and celebrate each other's successes, milestones, and everyday life. It's even about our four-legged family members who have stood by us and loved us unconditionally through some of our life's biggest challenges.

I see so many traits from my father in my son Michael. Dad had some interesting sayings (to say the least) and it's not unusual to hear one pop out of Michael's mouth. I cracked up when Michael told me about one of the first meetings he had had with a new boss. She excused herself to go to the washroom and out of Michael's mouth popped "Mention my name and you'll get a good seat." Good thing she had a good sense of humour!

I have two siblings, both brothers, one older and one younger. We are so different, in looks, personalities and traits. If you would ask each of us to describe the other I'm sure you'd get a totally different perspective.

My older brother Gerry is a brilliant surgeon. Growing up I was always amazed at how his mind would retain so much. He didn't have to cram for exams. Yes, he studied but he seemed to process information and remember everything he needed to do very well. His dream back then was to be a baseball player in the summer and a doctor in the winter. The baseball player dream never happened (professionally) although every spare moment he was out playing some sport or other with his friends.

As a kid, I was an acute asthmatic so sports wasn't really in the cards for me, but music was. I lived, ate and breathed music. I can't remember who we were talking to at the time but Gerry told him "All the artistic talent in the family went into Donna". I looked at him as if he was from another planet as he just didn't see how artistic he was in his field and his approach to everything he did. He always had his head screwed on straight, knew what he wanted and quietly went about doing everything he needed to do to achieve it; quietly that is except when it was exam time and then the obnoxious brother would come out. He'd pull my hair, or give me backwards (light) kicks or tap my shoulder from the other side and when I'd turn I'd have a finger in my cheek. It was easy to know when it was exam time. I tried to give him a wide berth (as if that ever worked!), although it was hysterical to watch the change in him.

When Gerry brought Karen home for the first time, we knew that she was 'the one'. She's a powerhouse in a small package and brought her own strong family values into ours. Friday night and holiday dinners are sacred to her as she brings the family together around the table to celebrate, and she does it beautifully. The table is always a work of art, her lists from holidays past, checked and checked again as she makes sure all the family favourites are represented and organizes everything that has to be done days and weeks ahead.

My younger brother Sheldon, Shelly as we fondly call him, is as deep as they come. He has a heart the size of the world, an innate sense of what's right and wrong and isn't afraid to share his opinion, although he's careful as to who he shares it with. He loves music and knows so much about the field. Radio truly is his home where he shines.

I am so proud of both of them.

There isn't a day that goes by when I don't speak with at least one of my family or extended family members. No matter where I am in the world I love to check in and see what's happening and to share what's going on in my life. I used to joke that if we sneezed in Ottawa, we got a "Bless you" from New York. The family network is that tight. Years ago, I remember asking my grandfather how it was he knew the moment we came home, as the phone would ring just as we walked through the door. He'd laugh and say "I don't. I just keep calling until someone answers so I know you're home safe and sound."

When I was at McGill, I would stay late into the early morning hours to practice as rooms and instruments were at a premium. Once we got the instrument we needed, we'd practice every second we could and well into the wee morning hours.

Sometimes, when a group of us would go to the Esquire Show Bar, a tiny dive of a place in downtown Montreal to take in a performance of one of the jazz greats of the time, I'd get home as late as 4:00 or 4:30 am. At 1:00 am they'd close the doors of the club and amazing artists like Dizzy Gillespie, Lionel Hampton, Chick Corea or Gary Burton would stay and jam with us music students.

When I got home, I'd take off the burglar alarm and then have to re-arm it. In those days we had to call into the monitoring station and tell them our access code. Everyone knew each other. Even the overnight alarm guy would lecture me and say, "Do you know what time it is? Why are you getting home so late? Do your parents know how late you've been coming home?"

We lived in a small suburb with its own police force, the station being around the corner and up the street. Sometimes a cop would stop me on the way home. It wasn't to give me a speeding ticket. The speed limit was 20 MPH (we hadn't gone metric yet) and at 3:00 am or later, I rarely did the speed limit when the roads were empty. It was to lecture me for being out so late. People had your backs. Life was more personal. I love computers and how they connect me with the rest of the world but I truly believe we have sacrificed a lot for the gains we've made.

The values I learned have stayed with me. Mom taught me what an open house really was. Our country house was always open to whomever knocked on the door. Way back when, when we had the guest house on top of the hill, it was filled with relatives and friends over the holidays. The fridges and freezer were filled with delectable baked goods that Mom made from scratch. The cupboard was filled with homemade raspberry jam, made from the raspberries picked from our own bushes in the garden. I can still smell the delicious aroma of the raspberries slowly cooking and thickening into jam. It was a bustling time, one I cherished, although I realise it wasn't easy for Mom as she was running, cleaning and cooking for two households.

Even though Mom had been a teacher and stressed the importance of education and working hard in school, she was also a talented artist, an amazing cook and baker and filled the house with colour, needlework, scrumptious food and welcoming warmth.

We still bake and cook up a storm for our family and friends who come for dinner or visit on the holidays. Meals and stories are shared, as is laughter and happy tears in the telling of them. Some of the mental snapshots are brought back by the scent of the snow-covered pines that wrap around the house, the smell of cinnamon and chocolate, slow-cooked briskets and Bubby's Honey Cake that fill our houses with the scents of home, present and past. All these years later you'll still find a new puzzle ready to go so anyone coming into the house can find that piece we'd been looking for, for what seemed like hours. Music, well, music is always a part of our home as we listen to oldies, hum as we putter, and all in all, create the space we need to enjoy life and make new memories to share in the future.

Dad taught me it isn't what you know as much as who you know. He was always a people person and people gravitated towards him wherever he went. He taught me that people enrich our lives beyond measure. It's all about relationships.

One thing I've learned through the years is that every person I meet knows something about life and living that I don't know. Whether it's the taxi driver taking me to the airport or the most brilliant professional, everyone has life experiences and lessons to share who I can learn from. I wish everyone would slow down to the speed of conscious life, to have those conversations with people we meet by chance and to check in with those close to us in our lives to share our accomplishments and celebrate life.

Dad had this desire to share his business experience and it was wonderful to see him advise Amy when she was starting her own business. His success in business was more about the relationships he created and cemented over time rather than a business model or the amount of money he made. He could sell you the Brooklyn Bridge not because he was a superficial, stereotypical salesman but because he always believed in what he was selling and connected with his customers in such a deep, profound and honest way.

My parents taught me great lessons over the years, some being:

- Life is not black or white, all or nothing;
- Do what really matters and make smart choices for how to use my time and money in the best possible way;
- Ask people to share their stories and learn more about life and living through their experiences;
- Continuously learn;
- Protect and cherish the 'space' I create in my life to live and enjoy life with those I love so we can create new wonderful memories;
- Never take people for granted;
- Look at everyday moments as extraordinary;
- Celebrate the small things as much as the huge ones;
- Let people celebrate your successes and remember to celebrate theirs;

- Pay attention to who's around you, what's around you and who and what you surround yourself with;
- The choices you make will determine what your future will be.

I learned to question things and to look at life through curiosity, recognising that I might not always get *the* answer, or the answer I want to hear. Sometimes we might not get any answers at all and have to live in the questions. That's OK too.

Most of all, I know that we can't keep people forever, no matter how much we might want to; so to cherish the gift of them in my life every day and let them know how important they are to me. I believe that is my best life lesson of all.

This is a glimpse of the past 60 or so years of life with my family from my own perspective. I know I'm skipping over a lot, but if I wrote everything it would be the never-ending book. I hope what I did capture triggers some great mental snapshots of your own, an inner smile, and a desire to continue to create wonderful memories in the making for you and yours. If so, I'd love to hear them.

Our house on Dufferin Road

1 DUFFERIN ROAD

I was fortunate that, unlike many of my friends, I didn't move from place to place growing up. I lived on Dufferin Road from the time I was born to when I got married and moved to Ottawa. For every memory there is a mental snapshot of a room or colour; containers if you will for the experiences to unfold.

There are so many memories of growing up there and in that neighbourhood. They are too numerous to write about, but here are some that really stand out for me.

I loved that house. It was as close to perfect as you can get. The layout was fabulous; the rooms open and bright. It defined open concept, something that is coveted in this day and age. It was a bungalow but as the back lawn was two tiered, the ceilings in the basement were high. There were windows around the perimeter, so it didn't feel like a basement at all. I remember Dad telling me about when he was one of the first people to get aluminum storm windows rather than the older steel ones that most people used back then. There were 52 windows of varying sizes and shapes.

The new aluminum storm windows were installed. A few days later a large truck went down the street and they all fell out and onto the lawn. Dad called the company, told them to pick up the windows, then called Rusco® and had steel storm windows installed instead. Last time we drove down the street, over 60 years later, those windows were still in the house and were looking good!

If you would ask me to describe the kitchen, I'd tell you that the layout probably rivals kitchen designer concepts even today. It was large and bright and had a ton of storage. For every item there was a perfect place to store it. There was a lazy Susan in the corner near the stove where my cousin Joyce and I used to hide. The laundry room and pantry were at the back of the house behind the kitchen. There was a broom closet in there that not only housed the broom, mop and vacuum but Dad's sock stretchers and, more often than not, a salami which hung by a string on a hook inside the door.

We had a beautiful rock garden in the front of the house that was planted with pansies, chrysanthemums, geraniums and other colourful flowers. Once in a while, when waiting for the school bus, I'd see an older man stop by the house, pick a flower and put it in his lapel. I'd run into the house to let Mom know the flower thief was back.

He never said a word to me. He'd just tip his hat, pick a flower, stick it in his lapel, then drive off. I found out he was an old friend of Grandpa's. He had this cool glass vial with water that attached to the back of his lapel behind his boutonniere buttonhole so the lapel flower would stay fresh all day. I was still angry at him for stealing our flowers, but he was a nice man, all dapper in his light-coloured 3-piece suit with a wide brimmed hat. He looked as if he belonged down south, not in Canada.

When I was a toddler I used to love to crawl into the kitchen in the middle of the night, open the lower kitchen cupboards, take out all the liquid dish soap, shoe polish, pretty much anything that was liquid and finger paint all over me and the kitchen floor. When that wasn't enough I'd walk in it in my sleepers and leave footprints all over the floor in Technicolor. My creativity was budding even that far back.

How did I get out of my crib to do that, you ask?

Well evidently I never liked to be confined and would find a way to climb out of the crib. I'd climb over the top, dislocate my shoulder way too many times and then find my way to where my creativity could find an outlet. Mom and Dad had extenders built on the top of the crib and extra bars added in-between and I still managed to climb out. Our pediatrician told my parents that if they didn't put me in a bed, I could have permanent problems with my shoulder.

So they put me in a bed.

That gave me even more freedom.

Where did I go?

Straight back to the kitchen.

Our housekeeper Mrs. Smithers, who I adored, would tell Mom to go back to bed and proceeded to clean me up from head to toe, then clean the kitchen from top to bottom. She had all the patience in the world for me.

Mom would keep telling me not to do that. As if that would ever stop me! She always said I'd look her straight in the eye, listen to every word she said and then would do what I wanted. It's not that I didn't listen. I did. I just didn't agree with everything she said!

We all loved that kitchen and as far back as I can remember, ended up playing in there, doing our homework in there and just hanging out. It was a huge room but very well laid out. The stove was fantastic. I would love to have one like that even today as it had 5 burners, two ovens, and two warming ovens. When I was a kid we would hide in the Lazy Susan in the corner, take out the Tupperware® and stack them and all in all, make a mess.

I remember Mom in her dresses and wedge high heeled 'play shoes' as she would call them. Later on I teased her that she was so perfect looking, she could have been in the movie The Stepford Wives. Not that she acted like one, she just looked, the part.

(Notice the infamous coffee maker on the stove.)

Gerry was probably the best behaved kid on the planet.

That's OK, I made up in mischievousness for the both of us. He was so good that when he woke up early in the morning before Mom and Dad, he would go play in his closet so he wouldn't disturb them. They found this out the hard way as they frantically scoured the house for him one morning, panicking, thinking he was missing. Then out walked Gerry as he heard the commotion and wondered what all the fuss was about.

Once I was put in a bed, Mom decided it was time to redo my room. I can't tell you exactly when that was. I do remember when they put wall to wall carpet in. It was a synthetic carpet, not easy to find in those days as most were made of wool, which I was allergic to. The carpet was a dusty pink. The furniture they bought was pink. the wall paper was flocked and pink on white, with pink marble end tables, pink everything! Even the china cat they bought for the room was pink.

I think there's a very good case for me hating pink even to this day.

After Shelly was born, Gerry moved into the front room which was a bedroom at night and a den during the day. It was a really cool room with two couches that converted to beds, built-in cupboards and drawers behind a moveable wall and a TV in the middle. One night, when I was a bit older, I wanted to do something as sleep eluded me, so I quietly sneaked into Gerry's room and went to turn the TV on. He was dead to the world so I figured I was safe. Remember the TVs with the pull on push off knob? Well I must have turned the knob all the way to the right maximizing the volume as I turned it on. There was this blast of static and a test tone.

He hit the roof! To this day he keeps asking me "What were you going to watch, an Indian head?" There was no programming at night when we were kids. I suppose it was before the age of infomercials and late night oldies.

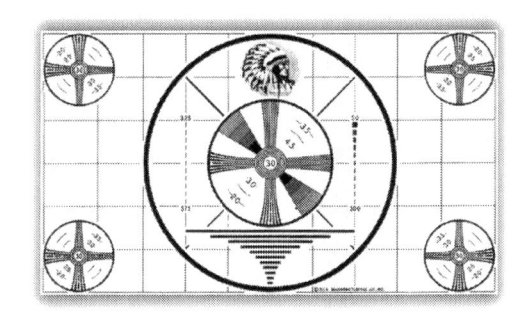

When I was four years old I started piano lessons. Grandma (Dad's mom) had decided that if my mother had a girl, she would buy back the piano her friend had bought for her daughter and refused to play. I don't know why I had to be a girl for grandma to do that but I suppose it was the way of things back then. Girls studied music and boys did sports if they were so inclined.

For my first present (not birthday but at birth), I got a grand piano.

Dad would sit with me and play chopsticks. I think that was his entire repertoire.

He would play for a bit, look sideways at me and start grinning. He was so proud of himself!

Over the years, lessons continued. My first teacher told Mom and Dad that she had taught me everything she could and recommended another teacher for me to work with. He kept entering me into competitions (which I hated). I had to practice every spare moment, before and after school, evenings and weekends to prepare. The minute I started practicing, all the doors would slam in the house.

Looking back and considering the atonal music my teacher kept giving me to play, I don't blame them. The selection of music I got to play was for the most part why I hated studying piano. Who studies piano for years and never gets to play even one piece of Chopin? Most of my friends learned the works of the Masters. That was never part of my repertoire.

The lessons and competitions continued until I was 16. By then I told my parents and my teacher that if he entered me in one more competition, I was quitting. I never believed that a panel of judges should interpret the music of someone who was not there or no longer alive and couldn't judge the execution for themselves. Who were they to tell me I was interpreting it correctly or not?

My teacher didn't listen and entered me in another competition. I won and then to no one's surprise other than his, I quit piano. My parents supported me in that decision. It was a huge weight lifted off me. No one should endure having to play a musical instrument. Playing should be an extension of our soul. The next day I applied to McGill for music performance in percussion. It was all because of the ripple effect of my brother Gerry who was a drummer in a rock band...

Gerry had a set of drums. Their band would practice in the garage so that it wouldn't be too noisy in the house. We had a forced air heating system. The sound went through all the vents and was piped through the whole house. I used to love watching them practice.

The band didn't stay together too long but the drums remained and were available.

When I entered high school all I wanted was to be in the West Hill High School band. It was one of the top bands in the province. But as an asthmatic, I was very limited as to what I could play. When I was asked if we had any instruments in the house, I said piano and drums. As there is no piano in band, I was given percussion.

Perfect!

We travelled to other parts of North America to compete with bands in other cities. We would be billeted with families of the band members in the cities where we visited and reciprocated when they came to Montreal. We travelled to Europe and went to 5 countries; Scotland, England, France, Belgium and Holland playing for royalty and in concert halls. What an extraordinary experience! When we came back, Mom and Dad invited the whole band over for dinner, ordered Kentucky Fried Chicken and we partied.

If my family thought practicing piano was annoying, they had a whole new outlook on things when I practiced snare drum. Still, I was good enough to audition for the music program at McGill and be accepted which was my dream, so it was worth it, to me at any rate. Anyhow, I digress...

Back in the day, we had a milkman and delivery man from the bakery who came to the house every morning.

I still have the 'SERVICE' sign from the milk man under the pillow on the bench from our home on Dufferin Road and one of the milk bottles.

If Mom wanted milk, eggs, butter or any other dairy item, she put a note in the milk bottle, put the 'Service' sign on the door the night before and everything would magically appear on the front stoop early the following morning.

Rain or snow, he was always there.

Then there was Solly the Baker.

He would come very early every morning with baked goods and freshly baked bread. The trick was that Mom had to get to the bread before Dad did or there would be trouble. He loved the 'shpitz', the hard crust on the ends. He would order unsliced round corn or pumpernickel breads and proceed to eat all 4 sides and the top and bottom. All that was left was the middle.

Mom was not impressed!

When I got older and we had our dog Columbo, Solly the Baker would scream "A stupid dog! I'm here every day and he doesn't know me?" Columbo would bark his guts out whenever he saw Solly. He might have been a beagle size but he was half German Shepherd and his bark was definitely 100% Shepherd.

Often times at breakfast, Dad would complain that there wasn't a cup large enough for his morning coffee. He wanted a huge mug, not the small cups from our dish set.

One day, on the way home from school, I passed Woolworths® and in the window was this HUGE English teacup. And I mean huge! It was meant to be a planter not a cup but hey, as Dad was always grumbling about how small the cups we had were, I bought it and left it by his place at the kitchen table with a note asking, "Is this big enough?" It must have held 2 pots of coffee.

I walked into the kitchen the following morning and there he was drinking from it. The coffee pot was empty. He was a happy camper — well until we absconded with the cup and relegated it to the dog. Dad on that much caffeine from a whole pot of coffee just wasn't a good thing on any level, so we gave him back his old mug and allocated the English teacup to Columbo for his water bowl. It has served as a water bowl to 4 dogs in two cities ever since, and the quest to find the perfect sized coffee mug for Dad continued.

Speaking of coffee, my parents had this old metal drip coffee pot. It had three chambers, the part on the bottom with the spout to pour, a middle section where you put the ground coffee and then the top where you poured boiling water which would drip through the coffee into the bottom chamber. Back in the day of more traditional percolators, this was quite innovative and happen to make amazing coffee — except one day.

Shelly wore glasses from the time he was a toddler. He hated wearing them. Mom kept the drip coffee maker in the lower corner of the lazy Susan cupboard which was definitely reachable for a toddler.

I knew that from personal experience.

One evening he decided to hide his glasses in the top of the coffee maker and then went to sleep. At the crack of dawn, as usual, Dad woke up and went to make the coffee. A while later, Mom came into the kitchen, poured a cup and tasted it and asked, "What did you do with the coffee? It's terrible!" Dad answered, "What do you mean? It's fine!"

In the meantime, Shelly woke up and Mom couldn't find his glasses. She tore through the house frantically looking for them as he couldn't see without them. Later that morning, Mom went to wash out the pot and there, in the top chamber, were two lenses, no frames.

The frames had melted.

Dad had drunk liquid plastic.

Off to the optometrist they went to replace the glasses. It's amazing we didn't have to have Dad's stomach pumped.

One evening Mom went to turn on the dishwasher. That in itself is nothing out of the ordinary, however when you put All® laundry soap in the dispenser instead of dishwasher soap, it's an event!

'Controlled suds' and 'active' were two prominent words on the label.

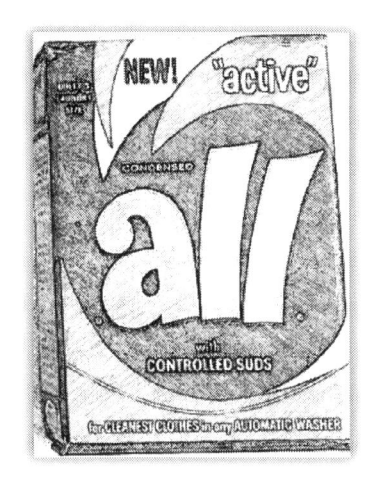

There was nothing controllable about those suds but they were very active as they started pouring onto the kitchen floor and down the hallway. There were bubbles everywhere!

Then there was the time when Gerry and I came home from school and heard water running.

We went downstairs where water was pouring out of the walls, everywhere! What would any kid do? We changed into our bathing suits of course and went to play in our 'indoor swimming pool'. Mom came home and heard the commotion downstairs and asked "What are you doing down there?" to which we replied, "We're swimming in the indoor pool!"

Mom screamed out, "We don't have an indoor pool!" then came running down the stairs.

The pipes had burst and water was pouring into our rec room.

We were thrilled! I can't say the same for Mom.

The house on Dufferin Road had fantastic acoustics. Before Shelly was born, Gerry and I would sleep in the two bedrooms on the side of the house, separated by a bathroom and huge double linen closet. The house had a forced air system which was perfect for acoustics and kids taking advantage of them them effectively.

We had a maid, Cathy, who Gerry and I didn't like, so what did we do? We acted like kids. We thought we could chase her away. Not that it worked but we still tried. When Mom and Dad would go out for the evening, we would whisper into the vents.

Sound traveled to the maid's room downstairs. We'd hear her march up the stairs and would run back to our beds and pretend we were asleep. She couldn't yell at us if we were sleeping (or so we thought). We'd stay very still with our eyes tightly closed until she would go back downstairs. The minute we heard her go back to her room, we'd start whispering into the vents again.

When Mom and Dad came home we would seem to be sleeping like angels. Cathy would scream and yell that we were taunting her and when Mom and Dad asked us what that was all about we played the innocents. She got fired eventually.

Mom had gone back to school to get her Master's degree in Special Ed. She had worked so hard that she came down with Mono and Hepatitis. She was very sick and was put on strict bed rest. That was the day that Cathy declared she was going to be stuck with too much work and rebelled.

Mom wanted to let her go immediately. Cathy refused to leave.

Mom called the police who went downstairs to escort her out of the house and found suitcases full of linens and other items she was trying to steal. We begged my parents not to get another maid. They didn't listen. But the next one we liked so we behaved, well somewhat.

When I was about 10 or 11 years old, I got the chicken pox. I was such a caring, sharing individual, I shared it with Dad so the two of us could experience it together. We were bed and home bound, although I bounced back faster than Dad did. He had a much more severe case than me and was really miserable.

One day in particular stands out.

Dad was in bed. I was in their room, playing on the floor next to the bed. Mom was out doing some errands. The doorbell rang and the cleaning lady went to answer it. There was a delivery of a magnificent basket of flowers with a get well note from Dad's friend Manny. She put them on the counter for Mom to see and went about her business.

Mom came home, went into the kitchen and saw the basket of flowers with a note saying "Water me" and proceeded to do just that.

She poured water over the flowers and then called out "Something moved!" She added more water which did the trick. It awakened a sedated chicken which had been hidden under the flowers. It jumped out of the basket and started running around the house with my mother chasing it.

That memory is indelibly etched in my brain. How many kids get to watch their mothers chase after a chicken IN the house?

The cleaning lady joined in, running with a pillow case to try to capture the thing, which she did. Mom called the butcher asking him to pick it up. He didn't want to have anything to do with it but what was my mother supposed to do with an old chicken? She called Dad's Uncle Peter to come and get rid of it. I think he brought it to a butcher who didn't want it either. I didn't ask too many questions as to what happened to it ultimately, but I have my suspicions...

I don't think they spoke to Manny for a very long time. We thought it was a riot.

We certainly didn't grow up in a boring house that's for sure!

When Gerry and I were both teens and, thankfully, we didn't have a maid any more, Gerry moved downstairs and took over the maid's quarters; almost like having his own apartment.

We decided to get our own phone line and share the cost. Back then one of the lines had to be a permanent connection and the other could be unplugged. I had the permanent phone and Gerry the one that could be unplugged.

By that time Karen was in the picture.

She'd call.

I'd answer because Gerry was already asleep (he wasn't a night owl like I was).

She'd ask "Did I wake you?"

She almost never did but Gerry? That was another story. I'd have to go downstairs, knock on his door and try to wake him up. When that didn't work, I'd have to shake him to let him know Karen was on the phone. You'd think he'd budge with the phone ringing next to his ear. He could sleep through an earthquake.

Many a time in the afternoon, I'd come home from school and the phone would ring. It would be Gerry's friend Chuck. When I'd tell him that Gerry wasn't home yet do you think he'd just leave a message? Oh no. I had to report to him what was new, what I was doing, how school was going, if I was dating anyone and anything else that occurred to him to ask. Even my parents didn't interrogate me like that. I think he knew more about my university days than my family did.

A few years later, Gerry and Karen got married. He left Dufferin Road and I moved downstairs. It was perfect. We had a two-line phone installed in the kitchen. It was one of those button phones. The button for the line that was ringing would flash. You'd push the button and answer. Simple!

I didn't have an alarm clock in my room and since Dad was up at the crack of dawn, I would ask him to wake me up at a specific time.

One morning, to wake me up, instead of walking downstairs he called my line.

The phone rang.

I picked it up and no one was there. That morning he called

me on my line, saw the button flashing on the bottom of the kitchen phone and clicked it to answer. Of course because he clicked the other line, his line hung up and all he heard was a dial tone.

All I heard downstairs was a dial tone.

I came upstairs to the kitchen and was about to ask him why he didn't even say good morning; that all he did was call and hang up. I don't think he had had enough caffeine at that point because before I could say anything he exclaimed "Someone called your line. I answered and they hung up on me!"

I shook my head and after asking Dad if he had had his morning coffee, said, "Uh Dad, you hung up on yourself. I think you need more coffee."

He had this sheepish kind of smile when he did something he was embarrassed about and there it was!

When I was in my later teens, Mom came home, walked into the kitchen where I was doing some homework and said "My lips are so chapped, I'm going to go put on some Blistex®. I'll be right back".

Except she didn't come right back so I went to find her.

I walked down the hall calling out, "Mom! Mom!"

There was no answer.

I walked into their room, walked around the corner, through the dressing room area into the bathroom where I found Mom looking in the mirror trying to pry her mouth open.

She had used eyelash glue instead of the lip balm and glued her mouth shut. Well, being a teenager, this was the high point of my teen years, but I was also smart enough to not tell her that because I'd pay for it big time.

I tried to help her but to no avail. We had to wait until Gerry got home from med school to figure it out.

He did.

I'm not quite sure how he did it, but whatever he did, worked.

Years after I moved to Ottawa, I received an email from an old neighbour of ours from our block on Dufferin Road. She was a couple of years older than me, so two grades ahead in school. We knew each other but weren't really close friends growing up.

I was quite surprised to hear from her and it was nice to find out what she had been up to. She had moved to Toronto after Grade 10 and I hadn't seen or heard from her since. We were going back and forth in emails and to say it was an enlightening conversation is an understatement. A part of it went something like this:

(G.P.) "We really lived in an 'interesting' neighbourhood".

(Me) " What do you mean? We lived on a pretty quiet block."

(G.P.) "Really?!! You've got to be kidding! You do remember that my father went to jail."

(Me) "Oh yeah! I remember that!"

(G.P.) "And a few doors down, our neighbour was arrested for drugs along with his friend next door."

(Me) "Oh yeah! I had forgotten about that one".

(G.P.) "And the family on the corner? Remember when the father was shot in the knee caps in front of his house?"

(Me) "No! I didn't know anything about that!" (Calling my mother) "Mom, did you know that Mr. S. was shot in the knee caps one day?"

(Mom) "We must have been in the country that weekend."

(Me) "MOM! That's your answer? That's all you've got to say? You don't sound at all surprised!"

(Mom) "Do you remember when Gerry went to their house one day and came home and said, "They must be very rich because they have a lot of telephones."? That's because he was a bookie."

(Me) "We lived in some neighbourhood. Why didn't I know about any of this?"

(Mom) "It was a long time ago." (Continuing the emailing.)

 (G.P.) "And you remember your neighbour across and down the street a bit? Her dad was friends with a notorious mobster from the U.S. who would come and visit. One morning I went over and had breakfast when he was there. My friend's mom put kippers on the table because he loved kippers. He pointed to them and told me to eat them. I told him no way was I eating that. My friend told me "If he tells you to eat kippers, you eat kippers."

I never went for breakfast again."

(Me, calling Mom) "Mom. Did you know who was visiting S.K.'s parents? (And told her the name of the mobster.) What did S.K.'s father do?"

(Mom) "He was in the carpet business."

(Me) "Did he roll people in carpets or did he manufacture them? WHAT KIND OF NEIGHOURHOOD DID I GROW UP IN?"

(Mom, laughing) "It was a long time ago". (The email with G.P. continued)

(G.P) "I felt bad for you because you were one of the most naive kids I ever knew. You really didn't have a clue about any of this, did you?"

Looking back I still can't believe it. Thankfully the rest of the people on the street were great but I will never, ever forget that conversation!

Our house in Lac Paquin

2 LAC PAQUIN

Scent-triggered memories....I remember when I wrote about that way back when. The scent of the snow-covered pines in Ottawa in our own backyard brings Lac Paquin to mind whenever I sweep the snow off the path. It was that fresh smell of the evergreens and pines in the air you would smell the moment we got off the highway and started on the small, winding road to our house.

Every weekend, every holiday, we went up to the country.

Montrealers didn't call it a cottage, it was a country house or "we're going to the country" but never "to the cottage." It's interesting how terms change from place to place.

Grandma and Grandpa had a large bungalow that was perched on the top of the mountain overlooking the lake. The view was spectacular. They had built on a large square den at the back of the house wrapped with wall to wall windows. That was the room we'd gravitate to. We'd play cards there, watch TV with them and go out on the back patio for BBQs.

On the side of their house, literally built into the side of the mountain, was a large stone patio with a wood fireplace, an oven, and a built in BBQ, although they used the charcoal BBQ at the back of the house more often than the one on the patio. Sometimes Dad would borrow a film from the owner of the theatre in Ste. Agathe and show these movies at night on the patio. That was usually for one of our birthdays.

Right by the side of the patio, there was a path with stone steps that went down to the lake. It was a great shortcut as otherwise we had to walk down the road all the way towards the gates, past the vegetable garden and to the dock. This was a direct route.

Grandpa had a bell installed on the side of his house. It was a huge bell that weighed a ton and could be heard at the lake or down the road. If Grandpa needed our caretaker Emile, he'd ring it once; twice for Dad. As he had a heart condition it was the best way for him to get hold of anyone back in the day before cell phones.

Our house was dark-stained pine wood with three red garage doors. The house was built into the side of the mountain down the road from Grandma and Grandpa's. My aunt and uncle had a place right across the road. Our cousins, who bought the guest house years later, were on other side of us up a steep stone walkway. It was a magical place.

In the winter, you could hear the crunch of the snow under the tires of our car as we slowed to make that last turn to drive through the red wooden gates. The moment we crossed that line, the rest of the world seemed to fade away.

People were always coming and going; family and friends visiting for the day, a weekend or longer. There was always a roaring fire crackling in the huge stone fireplace in the corner of the living room. Our caretaker, Emile, would come early in the morning, clean out the ashes from the previous day's fire and lay the logs for a new one. From the time we got in from the ski hill or from tobogganing or flying saucering, Dad would light the fire and keep it going until a couple of hours or so before we'd hit the sack.

We didn't rely on TV, although we had one; an old black and white. Video games and computers weren't around then, thank goodness. We'd be outside most of the day to come in to the roaring fire and a hot drink. My treasured pump organ was near the fireplace and I'd have fun trying to churn out a song or two.

We'd often go for a sleigh ride under warm blankets to bring the new year in. New Year's day we'd watch football or old movies; *Harvey*, the six foot three and a half inch rabbit, being one of my favourites.

There were books everywhere, needlework in all stages of completion that Mom and I did, a jigsaw puzzle in the works on the dining room table and cards, games, and of course music going most of the time. We were all avid readers so when one finished a book it went to the next one in line who called first dibs. On miserable days we'd have a fire going and you'd see many of us in our favourite corners of the couches, loveseats and chairs curled up with a page-turner.

I loved watching Karen. She was a physiotherapist back then so couldn't wear any nail polish while she was working. The moment she unpacked, she'd be sitting at the edge of the loveseat doing her nails on the small glass end table. Then she would be ready to settle in.

We'd cook up a storm, and if there was a jigsaw puzzle in the works, we'd lay the tablecloth over the puzzle very carefully so it could be lifted off, the puzzle waiting for whoever wanted to find that missing piece. It had a warmth, a sense of home that was felt the moment anyone walked through the door. Everything about it said 'welcome'.

In the summer we'd be down at the lake all day long if weather permitted.

The boathouse had a large red garage door and red trimmed windows with striped awnings over them. When I was a kid we had a couple of motor boats, a beautiful old wood one and a lighter and faster fiberglass one that Dad used when anyone wanted to go water skiing.

After a while the home owners around the lake decided it was too small a lake to have motor boats and for safety and pollution sake, banned motor boats. Dad sold the motor boats and bought two pedal boats. We already had a row boat and a canoe. Dad would love to go out on the pedal boat with a cocktail and take the sun. Gerry bought a license plate for one of them that said 'S. S. Pessie' in Mom's honour.

There was a small apartment upstairs with a balcony overlooking the water. I can't remember anyone ever staying there overnight but it was a favourite place of mine; somewhere I could go especially once the sun went down, lay on my back on the balcony, feeling as if I were suspended over the water. I'd look up at a gazillion stars blinking back. You could hear the odd croaking frog and crickets but little else. It was silent, a place where the troubles of our world would disappear.

The runoff from a cold mountain spring was on our property near the dock. Dad would load up the golf cart that we used to get around the property and carry heavy loads to and from the lake. He would fill up the trunk of the cart and bring soft drinks down and place them against the rocks under the cold running water to chill.

We'd fill our glasses with the freezing cold fresh spring water right from the runoff. Sandwiches and fruit would be kept in the cooler so we wouldn't have to go back to the house to eat or Dad would start the BBQ to grill down at the water. He made the best steaks. Moishe from Moishe's Steakhouse in Montreal, taught him how to pick the best meat and how to season it. Dad taught Gerry and me as well so the tradition continues.

It was idyllic. We would swim and go boating, just lay on a towel or chair on the dock or upper balcony of the boathouse and soak in the peace and quiet.

Every summer the vegetable garden would be planted with whatever would grow in that climate over a short growing season. Dad loved the shallots that grew almost to the size of onions. He would pick some on the way down to the water and wash the dirt off in the lake. Knowing what I know now about cooking, I would have loved cooking with the fresh grown garlic, beans, shallots and other veggies and would have had a field day with what we could pick right out of the garden.

We cooked differently back then.

My personal favourite was the raspberries growing on evenly spaced rows of bushes. They were so abundant that each of our households would have a huge bowl to eat almost every day. What we couldn't eat Mom would make into jam, not the jam that you put pectin in to thicken it with, but made the old fashioned way, cooking it slowly until it thickened all on its own.

When we wanted a break, we would go into Ste. Agathe to the movie theatre to watch something on the big screen. Back then there were two theatres, the Roxy and the Alhambra.

We would eat at Laurentian Bar, where you could get a smokeburger (Mom's favourite), sort of like a combination of a smoked meat sandwich and a burger. The sandwich was on a hamburger bun and then put on a griddle. They had the best milk shakes in the world and was a local gathering place. We would always bump into family or friends who were up in the country. Everyone seemed to gravitate there.

On the weekend, we'd sometimes treat ourselves to lunch at Au Petit Poucet.

They had the most mouthwatering maple syrup smoked ham sandwiches, beans with chunks of ham in it and hand cut fries. Oh and we can't forget their maple sugar pie…

When I went to camp as a counselor, I'd come back every day off. Sometimes I'd bring a friend and, more often than not, just grab a lift with someone who had a car so I could come home for 24 hours, catch up on my sleep, do my laundry and just hang out with the family. One day, I showed up early afternoon and saw a tent pitched on the grass near the shuffle board. I couldn't imagine anyone in our family sleeping in a tent! I shook my head trying to figure that out and went to drop off my stuff in the house. I heard some noise in the kitchen so took a detour to see who was there. It was someone I'd never seen before. He was at the fridge pouring a glass of milk. He turned from the fridge and before I could say a word asked, "Who are you?" to which I replied, "Who am I? I LIVE here! Who are you?" It was a friend of Gerry's from the hospital who loved to bird watch and asked if he could pitch a tent. It really was an open house — and property but it was the first time anyone had ever bird-watched there.

It was a place where no pressure, chaos, or crazy schedules existed, at least for us kids. We just had great times by the lake, walks in the woods, being with family and friends and enjoying whatever we did.

In the winter we'd ride on a toboggan or flying saucers, doing everything we could to not slide into the tree at the bottom of the hill by our aunt and uncle's house or we'd brave the cold and go for a walk. All you'd hear was the crunch of the cold snow under our boots.

We went for walks to the small country store for milk or our favourite soft drink, St. Jerome Nectar. We'd walk those extra few feet around the bend so we could see if the small waterfall in the creek had frozen over yet.

For years we'd wander down to the lake to skate when it was cold enough and some of the snow had been cleared. I'd often climb the hill to wake my cousin Mark up to go skiing, or try to. Waking him up was a feat in itself. We'd pile our stuff into cars and many of us would drive to the other side of the mountain to tackle the hills of Belle Neige.

We used to go skiing with Dad which was always a hoot. One weekend, when he was coming down the hill, the tip of his ski got stuck in someone's boot print and he took a bad tumble. St. John's Ambulance crew came to the rescue, had him X-rayed, told him it was a bad sprain and to elevate it. We put him sideways in the back seat of our station wagon and headed back to the house. We got Dad settled lying on the couch and as comfortable as he could be. We had a family doctor nearby in Ste. Agathe so my mother got on the phone to call Dr. Caron.

It was a fascinating conversation to say the least.

(Mom, calling the doctor), "Hello, can I please speak to Dr. Caron?

(Pause).

He's where? Africa? How long is he going to be there?"

(Dad, yelling from the couch in the living room), "I'm not waiting!"

(Mom, yelling back, covering the receiver with her hand), "I'm just curious!"

(Dad), "The hell with curious. I need help now!" And so it went.

Mom thanked the receptionist and quickly hung up. We debated as to what to do about the situation as we didn't know any other doctors in Ste. Agathe and decided the best thing we could do was go back into the city.

We piled blankets in the trunk of Mom's uncarpeted mint green Pontiac station wagon (no we won't comment on the colour) and lay Dad in the trunk so he would be flat. I'm not going to write what he said every time we went over a bump as it would be censored but suffice it to say, we finally got him home.

Having a son who was a medical student really came in handy. Gerry came home and surveyed the situation. "His leg should be elevated", he stated. He piled about 4 pillows at the end of the bed and tried raising Dad's leg onto them.

(Again the response has to be censored). Not only was it elevated but almost perpendicular to his body. Dad was not a happy camper. He not only survived the fall and sprain but Gerry's medical care. That was the end of his skiing days.

I thought I knew Belle Neige ski hill like the back of my hand. We skied there weekly on marked and unmarked trails. One weekend when Jeffrey was there we got an early start on the hill.

Jeffrey, being a gentleman, said, "After you!"

I went off a cliff.

They had bulldozed that unmarked trail away. That was the end of my skiing days. I ended up on crutches for 6 weeks which was really not convenient for running to classes on the wide-spread McGill campus in many parts of hilly, downtown Montreal.

We never had trouble sleeping, though Dad, being a firm believer of fresh air, would open the windows once we fell asleep. "It's healthy," he would say. We refused to get out of bed in the morning because healthy is one thing but practicing cryogenics to freeze us in time is another thing. Doing this in the summer time I can understand but in winter? In the Laurentians? In Canada? It was FREEZING!

We slept like logs in the country air, but try getting us out of bed to step onto the cold wood floor in the morning. We didn't want to budge.

We all screamed at him.

He kept doing it.

Mom would send Dad to Ste. Agathe to Richstone's Bakery to pick up TWO BREADS.

He got the bread — sometimes.

Sometimes he forgot because he was so busy buying the place out, from mini hors d'oeuvres to cold cuts, coffee cakes and everything else he couldn't pass up because it looked so good, he'd often have to go back for the bread! The owners of the bakery must have made their monthly sales quota each time he walked into their store. And the freezer downstairs kept filling and filling....

People were always coming and going. Even after I got married, we'd make the trek from Ottawa to Montreal and then after dinner drive up to the country or drive straight there if the rest of the family were already up North. It was worth the two and a half to three hour drive each way from Ottawa. We did that until June 11th, 1978.

I will never forget that weekend.

That was the day our country house burned down...

There was a power outage on the Quebec side where I worked so we were late coming in from Ottawa. I had to walk down 34 flights of stairs along with everyone else I worked with which took a while.

Karen and Gerry were moving to Columbus, Ohio for Gerry's

Fellowship. Howard, my nephew was two years old at the time. It was Karen and Gerry's anniversary so we were going to pick Howard up, bring him to the country with us and let Karen and Gerry have some quiet time and finish packing for their move.

By the time we got going, drove into Montreal and went to Bubby and Zaidy's for dinner, it was too late to pick up Howard and drive up North. We arranged to pick him up first thing in the morning and get an early start. As I usually did, I asked Dad to wake us up at 6:30 am so we could get going as early as possible. They no longer had the two-line button phone so he would come downstairs, knock on the door and be our alarm clock.

The next morning, not at 6:30 but at 4:30 am, he knocked and said "The house burned down".

He said nothing else, turned around and walked back upstairs.

I tried to get the cobwebs out of my head, wondering if I had heard wrong and was dreaming, hoping I had. I ran upstairs after him and found my mother in their room crying.

It was surreal. I still thought I was dreaming.

The house had burned down. The fire had been so intense, it burned the phone lines from that area to the main town and Emile had to drive into Ste. Agathe to get to the fire department. By that time the house had burned down to the garages and pretty much nothing else was left.

Dad insisted that if we had been there, our dog Columbo would have smelled the smoke and alerted us and they could have called for help. I was happy none of us were there as we could have all died in that fire.

One thing survived just by chance; our twin-spouted teapot.

Our Twin-Spouted Teapot

We had a few keepsakes from the house, thankfully one of them was our twin-spouted teapot which was present at the end of every meal and coveted by each of us.

For years before the fire every chance we had we'd visit all the pottery stores in our area of the Laurentians to see if anyone could reproduce this teapot. They all said no because it was a complicated design and not easy to replicate.

A couple of weeks before the house burned down we decided to check out potters and shops in Montreal so brought the teapot back into the city. Because of that, the teapot escaped extinction. Gerry and I were even more determined to find someone who could make one for each of us. We were sweet out of luck until one day, just by chance, a friend of mine told me that he had bid on something on eBay® and the whole site went down. eBay® had to reimburse many people for their bids. I thought I'd give eBay® a shot and check it out. I had never bid on anything before and figured I'd search for a similar teapot. I found one except the listing said it was only to be shipped to a winner from the United

States.

I wrote the seller a note begging him to ship to Canada if I won. He told me that if I wrote him why I wanted it so badly and my story was compelling enough, he would consider it. I wrote him about our country house, the fire, the rescued teapot and how Gerry and I had been searching for one for years. He was so moved, he agreed to ship to Ottawa if I won, and win I did! The one we had in the country was a pale yellow one. This was a cream coloured one in perfect condition. Gerry and Karen's dishes were cream so the first teapot was going to go to them.

I was so excited and couldn't wait to surprise them. I called Gerry and told him I had found a perfect birthday present for him. It was October and his birthday was in August. His response was, "My birthday was months ago. What is such a perfect present?", to which I replied "A teapot".

He hung up on me.

I called him back and said "THE teapot as in a teapot like we had in the country and in perfect condition! Is that not a perfect gift or what?" I had his attention. I think Karen was more excited than Gerry was about it. After months of searching, we became the proud owners of one as well, a gorgeous rich cobalt blue one to go with our blue and white kitchen.

Eventually I found one in the same colour yellow that we had in the country, except this one had some bands of gold around the lid. Now Michael and Amy have one with their names on it when they have space to keep it.

The tradition continues.

Indiana Jones

3 PETS AND SUNDRY

Growing up, since I was allergic to pretty much everything, we couldn't have pets other than the ones that swam or lived in a tank. As kids we had goldfish which lived in a tank in Gerry's room. I'm not quite sure whatever happened to them although I have suspicions...

Zaidy used to tell us all sorts of bedtime stories about these fictional characters so we name our goldfish after them: Fishel Flock, Pitsy Ritzy, Tseep Tsop and Uncle Ackachaynik. Many a bedtime story was created about them. They were the first and last fish that we had. Then we graduated to small turtles in a mini plastic oasis.

I would watch them endlessly as they walked up and down the little hill in the bowl to the plastic palm tree and then go back into the water for a swim. They were adorable. After a while we gave up on the turtles as they didn't have the longest life span.

A friend of Dad's, Algie brought us to a chicken farm one day and we came home with 2 eggs, a tiny incubator and all the trappings to hatch our own chickens. We would rush home from school to see how they were doing until finally the eggs cracked and out came two adorable chicks.

Unfortunately they didn't stay around for long, so that was the end of our pet stint for the time being.

When I was in my late teens, we came home with a dog from the Humane Society. We waffled as to whether to call him Banachek, Kojak or Columbo. You can tell what TV shows we liked to watch back then. It was winter and as we were walking down the street to give him a chance to do his business before entering the house, the pooch picked up a cigar butt he found in the snow. That made it easier. We chose to name him Columbo.

Columbo was half German Shepherd and half Beagle. He looked like a puppy Shepherd with floppy ears. He was the size of a Beagle but had the bark of a Shepherd (which Solly the Baker really loved....NOT!) As soon as we brought him into the house, he ran into my parents' bedroom and jumped on the bed, burrowed into my mother's pillow and went to sleep.

(Mom) "Get him out of my room and change the sheets!"

Within a week, he was curling up next to her on the bed with her stroking him down his back and my father begging him to come over to him.

He wouldn't.

When I was at school my mother was too nervous to leave the dog downstairs in the hallway next to my room. I was house training him. We put newspapers down in the hallway by my room. We left the bathroom door opened for light and to leave him some water. We kept the bedroom door closed so he could be in an area with a tile floor in case he had an accident. There was a door at the other end of the small hallway which we could close off to confine him to that small area until he was trained.

He didn't want to be there alone and knew my mother was in the house so would bark and yelp nonstop. Mom called Gerry to come over and study at home so he could be with her and the dog. Was Columbo on the path to being totally spoiled? Absolutely!

Dad loved this dog so much, he would come home from a wedding in a tuxedo, lie on the living room carpet and put Columbo on his stomach. He literally wore the dog in more ways than one.

One evening, when our cousins Ruthie and Lou were in town from New York, they all went out to this posh restaurant on the top of Place Ville Marie called Altitude 737. Dad found a phone on the floor under their table, picked it up, and called home.

Did he call to speak to me?

No! He called to speak to Columbo.

A couple at the next table were looking at Dad as if he were nuts as all he said into the phone was "Ticka, ticka, ticka" which was the sound he made when he tickled Columbo's stomach.

Did Columbo curl up with him when they got home? No!

Columbo was allowed to go pretty much everywhere except the white couches in the living room. He was smart enough to wait and go to lie there when everyone had gone out. How did we know he had been on the couch? The pillows were down-filled and the plumped cushions were indented with a touch of black fur left as a souvenir. One day Mom came home with cousin Ruthie who caught him in the act. Ruthie gave such a yell that the dog flew off the couch and the two-stair riser of the living room and hid in my parent's bedroom. His feet never touched the floor. I don't think he ever lay in the living room again in case Ruthie might have been lurking and catch him.

When we moved to Ottawa, they didn't allow dogs in our apartment. We originally moved for one year so I asked Mom and Dad to keep him until we got back. Did Dad listen to the instructions "Please only feed him dog food and no people food"? No.

I called home and asked how the pooch was doing and heard back, "It's Friday night. Columbo is eating chicken soup".

When we would bring him over to Bubby and Zaidy's I'd hear "A dog you need!" Within weeks, Zaidy quietly sneaked him some boiled chicken from the soup. He tried to do it secretly but the sound of the dog licking his lips and inhaling the food under the table nixed the secrecy in a hurry. Bubby would call the dog into the kitchen and say "Columbo, would you like an Aer Kichel?" It would take her hours to mix the dough and make these light cookies but she didn't hesitate for a second to give a few to the dog.

Dog food? Yeah right!

When we'd go to the country, Columbo knew who didn't like him. He would swim in the lake, saunter back onto the dock just up to my aunt and cousin Lynn who both hated dogs and proceed to shake and soak them. He did that every time. We tried not to laugh but couldn't help ourselves which got us into their bad books, regularly.

Columbo was the first of 5 dogs. He might have been a rescue dog but I think he rescued me. In some ways I think all our dogs did in some way.

When we brought Michael home from the hospital I knew it was going to be a long and difficult journey ahead. About three weeks after Michael was born, he went for some nerve conductivity tests which were hell on earth. When we got back to the house, I handed Michael to the baby nurse, went into our room so I could call Gerry for advice.

Columbo sensed that I was having a hard time. I sat cross-legged in the middle of the bed speaking to Gerry about what the neurologist had said. All Columbo saw was that I was home. He wanted to play. I just sat there talking to Gerry ignoring him so he jumped off the bed and brought back his ball.

I still ignored him.

He jumped off and brought another toy, then yet another, and another until all his toys and bones were in a pile in front of me. When I still didn't react, he knew something was very wrong, moved right up to me, sat down, put his paw on my shoulder and stayed like that the whole time I was on the phone. He was the smartest dog I ever had and was loved by all, well, maybe except by Shelly...

When Michael was post-op in the hospital in Montreal, we got a call from Shelly that Columbo had bitten him and he had to have a tetanus shot. He was going to go to the Herbert Reddy Hospital next door and then drop by the Children's Hospital to see us.

He walked into the room limping. The shot wasn't as bad as his embarrassment when he had to drop his pants to get the injection. He walked down the block to the Children's Hospital afterwards really angry, came to Michael's room and sat down then promptly popped up because of the pain in his butt.

Mom and I were puzzled. We asked, "Didn't Columbo bite your hand?" to which he answered, "He did, but I had to have the shot in my butt at the hospital and that's killing me!"

We laughed so hard we almost fell off our chairs. That didn't make Shelly very happy. He didn't "talk" to Columbo again for a long, long time. I don't think he talked much to us for a while either.

After Columbo we had a variety of dogs, all with their own ways of worming themselves into our hearts.

Our next dog was an inherited one. Our electrician's wife had just passed away. He had three little girls and a dog and couldn't handle any of it. He begged us to take Sandy, promising she was a sweet pooch. We couldn't say no, so the next day, we had a new addition to our family. She was a Lab / Husky mix. She was very pretty but definitely not well behaved.

Sandy was an escape artist. She found a way to get out of our fenced yard every chance she could get and I'd have to roam the streets of Ottawa to find her. When she stayed in the house, I'd come home to an opened closet and would find only my left shoes chewed. I'd put her in her punishment spot near the buffet in the dining room. After the first couple of times, where would she be when I got home from work? In her punishment corner as if to say, "I'm already here. What are you going to do about it?"

She was really smart but a problematic pooch. We looked for a new home for her and found one with a psychologist who lived on a farm. Perfect! No fences for her to escape from and someone to analyze her temperament.

After Sandy we decided to go for a purebreed and chose to get a Golden Retriever. I wanted an American Golden which tends to be a lot darker than English Golden Retrievers. A friend pointed us in a direction of a breeder not far from Ottawa. We drove out to see the dogs and picked a pup. We had agreed to pick him up right after we were back from Norfolk, Virginia and Michael's pre-op. The deal was that if we could find a pup, house train him and be able to board him before Michael's next surgery, we would bring one home. The timing worked perfectly. The hardest part was trying to figure out how to tell Mom we were getting another dog.

Soon after we picked out our pup, we were in Montreal. We had had dinner at Gerry and Karen's and when we got back to the apartment, there was a power outage. We had to walk up 22 flights of stairs to Mom and Dad's apartment.

Dad was out of town. Mom was totally exhausted from the walk up to the apartment and was listening to the news on the transistor radio to see if there were any updates for when the power would go back on. She was lying sideways on their bed listening to the reports and said breathlessly, "I can't talk. I need to catch my breath."

I responded, "Great! You won't be able to scream at me when I tell you we got another dog!"

She gave me that 'Mom look' and didn't say a word — at least then, but later? That was a different story!

Figment of Your Imagination, better known as Figgy was our next family addition. Michael loved the Dragon character from the Kodak Pavillion at Epcot and so named the pup after him. He was the colour of figs or a dark cognac with amber coloured eyes. He was stunning, an unusual colour for a Golden Retriever.

He did leave his mark on Dad. When we were visiting Mom and Dad in a place they rented in Killington, Vermont one summer, Figment bit Dad's nose. We ended up in the emergency room so Dad could have a tetanus shot and get some stitches. Dad didn't listen to us when we told him that Figment wasn't Columbo and you couldn't do a walking up his nose thing with your fingers, his face in Fig's face, going "ticka, ticka, ticka". He found out the hard way.

Figment wasn't healthy from day one but we thought he would get better. After 7 weeks in and out of the veterinary hospital and only two and a half years old, we knew it was a lost cause. He was suffering. So that was it.

I think I cried for 7 weeks as he was being tested and ultimately, as he couldn't keep food down and had too many medical issues, we had to put him down.

I vowed never to get another dog again. But leave it to Michael. He wanted one and figured that emotional blackmail was the best way to get one.

When we were in Norfolk, Virginia for his pre-op testing, he refused to lie down for a CT Scan until I promised I would get him another dog. The nurses ganged up on me and said "Promise you'll get him a dog so he can have the test!"

What's a mother to do?

Welcome another Golden Retriever, Indiana Jones (notice the water bowl?).

Michael had a knack for naming dogs.

Why Indiana Jones?

Because he was so mischievous that Michael said our house would become the Temple of Doom.

He was a sneak, adorable as a pup and a gorgeous dog. He guarded Michael with his life, especially after his surgeries. He was a delight. He got me through some very rough times. No matter what was going on, I'd wake up laughing because of his antics.

A few years after we got Indy, and pending divorce, I was on my own with Michael. By this point there was no furniture in the master bedroom and I was sleeping in the guest room. There wasn't enough room for Indy on the smaller bed so he got pretty annoyed with me. He'd sleep on the floor parallel to the bed and if I had to get up in the middle of the night I'd inevitably trip over him as his fur blended in with the colour of the hardwood floors.

Finally, about six months later, I decided to get a new bed for the master bedroom and move back in there. I was so proud of myself that I put the frame together and got the bed made and ready to try out that night.

What I hadn't done just yet was put the rubber coasters under the wheels of the feet of the bed.

Indy looked in the room, saw a bed in the middle of the floor and thought to himself, "Great! I have a bed again!" and ran to jump up onto the new bed.

It rolled across the floor and into the wall with this 4 legged hairball digging in with his paws for dear life. It was straight out of a cartoon.

Once the bed banged against the wall and stilled, Indy jumped off and wouldn't go back on it for weeks.

I thought, "Yay! I have a bed all to myself!" I think the moment those thoughts ran through my mind he discovered it had been anchored and took over most of it. You don't fight with a 92 lb. dog of solid muscle. He would start the night off by lying diagonally across the bed which meant my feet had to hang over the side. I couldn't budge him. Thankfully in the middle of the night it would get too warm for him so he'd relocate to the floor.

He'd lie on the hardwood floors in the hallway, on his back, with his legs climbing up the wall. It was a riot to see it and, even better, I got my bed back.

Indy loved to go for his runs in the morning and when the weather was good enough, a swim in the small lake near our house. He was an early riser and wanted to get going in the morning so did everything he could to wake me up. If it was a weekend, I'd want to sleep in a bit. That never worked.

First, Indy would quietly jump on the bench at the foot of the bed, sit and watch to see if I stirred at all. When I didn't, and staring at me didn't work, he'd walk right up to the head of the bed, sit and look down at me. If that still didn't work, he'd take his paw, grab the sheets and strip the bed in one fell swoop. If I caught the sheets before they hit the bottom of the bed or the floor, he'd whack my head with his paw.

If that didn't work either, he'd leave. Being half asleep, I'd be lulled into a false sense of security that he was letting me go back to sleep for a bit.

Nope.

He would leave, find his prized possession, a softball he found in the field on one of his walks, come back onto the bed and bombs away!

He'd drop the ball on my head.

Who was the Smart Alec who named that thing a softball? There is nothing at all soft about it!

Indy was my shadow. When he died, half the neighbourhood came to say how sorry they were. Even the older teenagers would ring the bell just to say hi to Indy on Halloween and, after he died, to come and tell us how much they missed him.

Actually, on one Halloween, when Michael was too young to go out on his own, Indy and I accompanied him 'Trick or Treating'. We stayed on the sidewalk while he walked from house to house.

At one house around the corner, my friend's mom answered the door and asked Michael, "Are you all by yourself?"

Michael answered, "No. I'm with my brother."

She said to him, "I didn't know you had any brothers or sisters. I thought you were an only child."

He pointed to Indy and said "There he is!" I had no idea how to respond to that but knew I would have to have an important conversation with Michael when we got home.

Indy loved Mom and would curl up half on top of her every time they were together. She loves wearing black and would end up 'wearing' half of his fur. She would complain about it, but would constantly pet him as he lay tucked up against her.

Dad would beg the dog to come to him.

He wouldn't.

That seemed to be a trend for all our dogs...

When Indy got sick and we had to put him down, it was devastating and again I vowed never to get another dog. He died the day before Halloween. It was a warmish day and, as a distraction, I went outside to rake the leaves off the front lawn. Indy would have been out there with me.

Our next door neighbour Hank was outside raking as well and asked where Indy was. I told him what happened. He ran inside to tell his wife Phyllis and break the news. She came over to tell me how sorry she was. The neighbour next door to them heard what was going on and ran inside to tell his wife. They came over to tell us how badly they felt. And then it spread to the neighbours next door to them.

And so it went.

The kids who came trick or treating wanted to know where Indy was. He was always front and center as we dished out the loot. Everyone loved him.

Michael and I packed up all his food, treats, toys and such and walked it around the corner to our friends' house and the home of Indy's girlfriend Shawna, another Golden Retriever. Shawna was so comfortable in our home that if I was at the door speaking to someone and she heard me from the field across the street, she'd tear over here, come into the house, run upstairs, jump onto the foot of the bed, curl up and go to sleep. Not only was our neighbourhood like one happy family, our dogs were close as well.

After one of Michael's surgeries, he tried talking me into getting another dog but didn't win that time. We were sitting in the den watching the Madison Square Garden Dog Show on TV. On came a Bernese Mountain Dog. He was gorgeous, and huge!

Michael looked at the dog and said, "Mom, could we look at Bernese instead of a Golden Retriever for our next dog?"

"Michael", I answered, "We are not going to have a 'next dog'. Besides which this one is as big as a horse".

(Michael) "They have a great temperament".

(Me) "I'm sure but we're just not getting another dog never mind a Burmese".

(Michael) "Mom, it's Bernese as in Berne, Switzerland, not Burma".

(Me), "No way can I have a dog called Bernice and if it's a male, Bernie. Our cousin Bernie wouldn't be happy about that."

(Michael) "Mom, we don't have to name it that!"

(Me) "No dogs!"

The next day Mom and Dad drove to Ottawa to see how Michael was doing post-op. The finals for the dog show were on.

Mom looked at the winner which was the Bernese Mountain Dog and said, "What a gorgeous dog!" to which Michael replied, "I know. That's the breed I want to get."

(Mom) You want to buy a horse? He's the size of a horse!" Donna, tell me you're not considering it."

It was close, and we considered it until we heard about the complications that breed has and then decided to have a hiatus.

That was it for dogs at least until Ray entered my life, and with Ray came Toby. He was the most adorable dog, deaf as a doorknob with congestive heart failure, but cute? He had us wrapped around his big fat hairy toes.

Mom and Dad didn't even give me the "What do I need a dog for!" lecture with Toby. The consensus was, "He's adorable" and that was the end of that.

He could usually be found in his 'treat corner'.

His hairy toes didn't help as he would slide backwards until he hit something to stop him from slipping. You'd hear the Toby shuffle. Slide, slide, slide, scramble to get his feet back under him.

One day he slid under the telephone table chair near his treats and stayed there. It was a perfect fit. Not only could he give us his Toby look that said, "I'm good. I deserve a treat!" but he stopped slipping and sliding.

At night, as we got ready for bed, he'd walk over to my side of the bed, sit down, try not to slide and look at me as if to say, "Elevate me." He wanted to get up onto the bed and relax and was too small to jump that high. He had his own bed in-between the bureau and the dresser but always started off at the foot of our bed.

We had a special cloth on top of the covers so that he wouldn't get the bedding full of dog hair. I'd go into the bathroom, telling him to lie down and not go to the pillow. I'd come out of the bathroom and there he would be, lying on my pillow. I'd look at him with my hands on my hips. He'd look at me without moving his head an iota as if to say,

"Yeah, like make me move!".

I'd point him back in the direction of the cloth at the foot of the bed and, like a good pup, well most of the time, he'd go without an argument.

When it was time to shut the lights, he'd pop up as if to say, "Time to go down to bed. Come help me."

And we did.

He'd snore away, whimper in his dreams and was a presence even when he was fast asleep.

R. I. P. our hairy-toed pooch. We miss you.

SNIPPETS OF MEMORIES

SECTION E
FOOD
Make that snow go!
Get smokin'
Comics
E6
Lovely latkes
Make them as simple or as elaborate as you like. These are side dishes with a difference
See LATKES on page E6
Donna's Favourite Potato Latke

4 HONEY CAKES, HOT DOGS, LATKES AND MORE
(And a bit of sidetracking here and there)

Our family is known for tradition. When we stray from a menu even for one holiday we are collectively screamed at. We might try a new recipe here or there but ultimately, with all the protests, traditional favourites reappear on the table.

Bubby's Honey Cake is always front and centre for every occasion and is a staple in all our family's households. Many of her recipes were sought after and we would beg her for lessons.

One weekend, soon after I was married and back in town, I asked Bubby if she would teach me how to make her Giyourna. That was one of her specialties. It was a sweet yeast dough, rolled with butter, cinnamon and brown sugar and topped with pecans, more brown sugar and butter and made in a large tube pan.

For the longest time Bubby made one without raisins for our house, as Dad preferred it raisin-free, and made the rest of the Giyournas studded with raisins. For the grandchildren, she would cut the dough into smaller, individual Giyournas, until they had their own kids and would graduate to the full-sized version.

Sunday morning I reported bright and early to Bubby's for a Giyourna lesson. Little did I know how much work it would be. Everything was made by hand and once she made Giyournas, she would make them for everyone.

We had to knead each batch of dough about 300 times. We made three large ones and countless small ones. That meant bowls and bowls of dough which had to rise. She would put them on the couch in the den, covered with towels. That was the warmest room in the house. It took hours to make them all but it was well worth it. They might take half a day to make at the very least but would take about a minute to inhale. The experience of taking that first bite was indescribable.

One of Bubby's famous dishes was her beef borscht. She used to put it up in a special ceramic crock and let it ferment like good wine. She would start it at Purim, a month before Passover. She'd choose the oldest beets to use, cover them with cold water and for four weeks, let them sit, skimming off the top now and then. Two days before Passover, she'd cook it with some fresh beets and some beef flanken, season and simmer it.

Karen has kept up the tradition. She makes it in 3 large jars, so each family has some for the holidays. As Auntie

Charlotte and Uncle Saul would be with us for the first Seder, they would have the borscht with us. Once we split up and had separate Seders, whoever was hosting the Seder for Auntie Charlotte's family would get the Borscht.

Years ago, Uncle Solly would call Karen five times or more a day to ask her about the Borscht.

"Did you put up the Borscht?" was a question he asked every year.

One year, he called what seemed like 100 times. At the Seder, when Karen asked who was going to have Borscht, Solly put up his hand and said, "I'll have chicken soup."

We thought Karen would take a fit.

She looked at him, her hands on her hips and exclaimed, "You called me 100 times a day to ask if I had put up the Borscht and you want chicken soup? Well you're getting Borscht and that's that!"

And that's what he had.

Every household or family has their all-time favourite dishes and so many memories attached to them. I was sitting with mom and my brothers asking them what they remembered as their own favourite meals growing up. It went from, "I can't remember that far back" to "Oh, I do remember… " and the list grew and grew.

Mom had her specialties as did our grandmothers. Mom's meat pie (Which Ray insists is called Shepherd's Pie) was mentioned by all. It wasn't only that it was the best version of this household staple I ever had, but it had to be eaten in a specific way. It would be dished out in a perfect square, a meat mixture topped with corn and fluffy potatoes, but once it was on the plate, it had to be squished down with a fork so it would reach to the edges of the plate. Then slowly it would be eaten from the outside edge inwards. I think she taught us to eat it that way so it would cool faster and not burn our mouths, but that too became a tradition.

Other specialties of Mom's mentioned were her sweet and sour meatballs, apple sauce, icebox cookies, brownies with marshmallows in-between the squares and the icing and so on. Actually all Mom's squares were legendary.

Dad was the expert steak griller. He knew how to choose the best steaks, season them and grill them to perfection. That's something that was passed down to the next generation.

The smell of apple sauce simmering or a brisket cooking in the oven, or even more lethal, mom's prime rib coated in a mustard crust was so mouthwatering that we had to leave the house. The smell made us so hungry it was torture.

I asked Gerry if he remembered Eggs in a Hole or Eggs with Birdies. He thought it was Mom's way of getting us to eat eggs. He's probably right. Shelly certainly remembered them. Those were two of the dishes he immediately mentioned off the top of his head.

Shelly's favourites included lokshen and cheese, a noodle dish Mom used to make, and her rice pudding was up there on his list, but I think his overall favourite food group was breakfast cereal.

In those days Mom would call in her grocery order and have it delivered. As soon as she'd call they'd say, "Oh the cereal lady!"

Shelly had an array that he would choose from and to this day can rattle off the list: Cocoa Puffs®, Frosted Flakes®, Honeycomb®, Alphabets®, Lucky Charms®, Sugar Crisp® and Trix®. Good thing we had a large pantry! And to quote Shel, "If we knew then what we know now about sugar..."

I can still picture Shelly looking for words in his bowl of Alphabets...

A definite family favourite was hot dogs. Dad thought hot dogs was the best food group ever and loved to find the best hot dogs and the best hand cut fries in every city he visited. Every year before Passover, whoever wasn't busy preparing for the Seder would pile into the car and go to Lafleur's for steamies and fries.

Even after Dad passed away, the kids went to Lafleur's before his funeral to celebrate him in a way he would have loved.

He'd come to Ottawa and say "I'm going to take you out for the best lunch," and we'd end up at Costco for one of their huge dogs. I'd love to listen to Dad and Amy discuss the merits of the food trucks in Ottawa; who had the best hot dogs and who had the best fries and compare notes. They agreed on some but not on others but listening to them discuss this was a scream in itself.

Shelly on the other hand had his favourite haunts for hot dogs or burgers and fries. His absolute favourite place was Curb King on Decarie Blvd. before the expressway was built.

I'd take him there for a quick bite as a treat and we'd have some quiet time. Sometimes he'd choose A & W instead but those were 'our places' where only the two of us would go.

His 'special place', when he was a kid, was Piazza Tomasso more because he loved Magic Tom than the food I think. There were many places that we enjoyed going to as a family, from Miss Montreal to Pumpernicks, Snowdon Deli, and Ruby Foos.

We all loved eating at Ruby Foos. Mom loved their Pu Pu platter and their croque-en-bouche, a tower of cream puffs held together and surrounded by spun caramel.

It was a special place restaurant where we celebrated many a birthday or milestone.

When I was about to get on a plane for the first time to go to Europe with the band, my boyfriend took me to Ruby Foos for dinner to wish me a great trip. After dinner, a cake arrived at the table with "Bon Voyage!" written on top.

I looked at my boyfriend as the waiter walked with it to the table and before I could say anything he shook his head and said, "It wasn't me. I didn't order it."

The waiter pointed to the next table where brothers Rocket and Pocket-Rocket Richard were having dinner. They told me that they overheard our conversation and wanted to wish me well on my trip. I thanked them and told them that the only way I would accept it was if they would join us for coffee and a piece of cake.

To my utter delight, they joined us and we had dessert with two hockey stars from my childhood! That was an evening I will never forget. I can't remember what we talked about. I think I was star-struck.

I certainly can't leave out Mr. Steer for some of the best burgers and curlicue fries.

We'd go there from McGill or on weekends with a group of friends and talk for hours. It was close enough to school that we could be in and out in-between classes. For years after I moved to Ottawa, we would go back there and have lunch.

Many of the conversations I had had would come to mind and bring back some amazing memories of my time at McGill.

Then there's the Orange Julep.

That place is a Montreal institution.

We'd go with Mom and Dad, with friends from school or after camp to see some of our campers. I have so many great memories of that place!

One that especially stands out was when Dad had picked me up from somewhere and, on the way home, took me for a

Julep and a dog. He had just had his car washed.

At the O.J. they would come to your car and put the tray of food on a half lowered window. When you finished you'd toss the cups and wrappers on the ground and they'd pick them up and throw them out.

Well one day I couldn't finish my orange julep and as always, tossed the cup out the window. The thing was the window wasn't lowered.

We watched the pulpy drink slide down the window and into the door. Dad was not a happy camper! As Shelly would say, It's amazing I survived childhood.

Some of our old haunts are still around and others not but the memories still stay strong.

We learned a lot about cooking and holiday celebrations from our parents and continue many of the traditions, adding our own over time. One of these traditions is making potato latkes for Hanukkah.

I used to write a food column and was featured on the front page of the Ottawa newspaper for my specialty recipes. The photographer had to snap pictures very quickly because the editor was popping the latkes so fast they were almost gone before they were captured on film.

Believe it or not, making great latkes is not so easy. Each of us has our own recipe and method of making them, but one mistake could relegate them to the trash bin. We take latke making very seriously. So much so that at one point, the latke discussion traveled the world, from Montreal to Amsterdam, to Kingston, Ontario, to Ottawa and finally to

Norwich, England and back.

If you ever wondered why I am the way I am, read this and you won't wonder any more.

Our family latka saga...

Some background...

Joyce, is my first cousin and like my sister. We have the same voice (our mothers can't tell us apart), we both love to cook and we laugh, talk, tease each other and share everything whenever we're together which is never enough.

Steven is her younger son, living in Kingston and he and my son Michael have always been close. Lauren is Joyce's niece who is around Michael's age.

OK — now the latke recipe saga — It's long but worth it.

To: Donna
From: Joyce
Subject: How to make potato latkes

Dear Donna,

Lauren was in Amsterdam for a semester and asked me to email her my recipe for potato latkes. The funniest part for me is that I looked up a recipe for potato latkes in *Second Helpings*, and the instructions are 2 short lines!

Love,
Joyce

From: Lauren
To: Joyce
Subject: Hi

Hi Auntie Joyce,

How are you?

On Friday we are going to Switzerland for the weekend. We are going to check out where Daddy went to school. When we get back we are making a Christmakkah party. I told them that I would be in charge of the potato latkes...the only problem is that I don't have a recipe! Sooo...I knew that you would have a delicious one! If you have a recipe, can you send it to me please?

Miss you and love you lots!

Lauren

From: Joyce
To: Lauren
Subject: Re: Hi

Hmmmmmm......

Potato latkes is a recipe that is better discussed, but I will try to write it.

I will put all the ingredients in BOLD to make it easier. Read the whole thing before you start doing anything. This step is very important.

Take some potatoes.

Lots is best.

Even if you think you have enough, add some more.

When you are finished peeling, look at them and think very seriously - Do I have enough?

Then go and get one or two more potatoes and peel them too.

You should be peeling them into a large bowl - or pot if you don't have a large bowl.

If you don't have a pot or a bowl….use the sink.

Fill it up with enough water to cover the potatoes.

Add some salt.

Even 1 Tablespoon.

Then you have to start grating.

If you don't have a processor and you have to grate these potatoes by hand, put back at least half the potatoes that you took out in the first place. Then you can start with the onions.

Don't put any mascara on before working with the onions. Your face will turn black when your eyes start tearing and it won't look good to Matty to see black tears dripping down your cheeks. Even if it doesn't bother Matty, I am sure you will not feel like taking off all your makeup and reapplying it for nothing.

Okay, back to the onions.

They could be chopped to smithereens in the processor, or grated by hand. If you grate them by hand, be prepared for Niagara Falls-sized tearing. Be careful not to let your tears fall into the onions.

How many onions, you may be wondering? Good question.

There actually is no definitive answer.

Steven likes to use lots.

I probably use 1 medium onion to 4 or 5 medium potatoes.

**Important. Don't grate the onions right on top of the potatoes.

If the potatoes sit - even a little, they do 2 things.

1. They turn brownish --- that's not a pretty sight. If the grated pieces are large, I put them in a colander and run cold water on them. If you don't have a colander or a strainer, squeeze out the water.

2. The potatoes give off water - drain them by squeezing into a colander or sort of picking up the extra water with a large serving spoon.

Now you can mix the onions and the potatoes.

Now add the eggs, salt, pepper, flour.

I'm sure you're wondering what the quantities should be.

Hmmmmmmmm.

Eggs - beat them a little separately before you add them. I am guessing when I say use 1 egg for every 4, 5 or 6 potatoes.

Just add a little flour. I would say not even 1 tablespoon per potato - maybe a teaspoon per potato makes more sense. I don't know if that helps.

The batter should be battery - not too thick or loose per se, but the egg sort of makes it hold together. Try picking up some batter with a large serving spoon. The middle should be able to hold itself a little higher than the outside. Add an extra egg or two if you think you need it. It really does not need a lot of flour, but as you go along frying them, you could add a little extra flour if you think you need it.

Add some salt and some pepper. More salt than pepper.

Then mix it all up.

Wash your hands.

Put a finger in the batter, and taste it to see if you have enough salt. Wash your finger off before you put it back in the batter again!!!!!!

Don't take too long doing all of this, because in the meantime, your potatoes are turning brown and more water is accumulating - get rid of the extra water as it develops.

You need a good fry pan.

Use a good amount of oil - not just a little drop covering the very bottom of the pan.

If you want the latkes to taste good, use enough oil.

Make sure the oil is hot before you put any latkes in the pan.

Use a large spoon to pick up the batter. Lower it gently and I am not joking when I say to be careful. Oil splatters and you really have to protect your eyes. Seriously. I almost got a splash of oil in my eye once and it was very frightening.

Make sure the heat is high enough but not too high.

You don't want the potatoes to burn.

The heat should let the latke cook through to the middle and have the outside brown.

Then turn it over and do the same on the other side.

It is better to turn the latkes over only once.

Make sure they are nice and brown and crispy.
Place them on paper towels to drain.

Don't eat them too quickly or you will burn your mouth.

Love,
Auntie J

P.S.

Are you ever going to ask me for a recipe again?????

From: Joyce
To: Steven
Subject: Here is an email I sent to Lauren.

Love,
Mom

From: Steven
To: Lauren

I will add some comments, most of them from lessons learned in the last several years of latke cooking.

QUANTITY

Potatoes, once grated, take up more much space than potatoes pre-grating. When you evaluate the quantity, keep that in mind.

Also, it sounds like there will likely be multiple foods there, so be careful not to go off the deep end with quantity.

I provide these warnings mostly due to the effort and time to grate by hand if that's the way you're doing it, which I assume (peeling takes time too).

Also, unless you've got access to multiple frying pans, cooking takes time too.

But latkes are good, so more is good, and leftover latkes are good too.

Expect it to take time regardless of quantity (you may be surprised how long it takes for something so relatively simple), but it's worth it.

ONION

Use lots of onion - more is better. A lot of the flavour is from onion, and at your age it shouldn't cause you too much grief (I'm still safe from onion, though that probably jinxed me).

I usually think - holy &#% that's a lot of onion (or something to that effect), and it's never been too much.

I would probably go with 1 onion for every 2 or 3 potatoes (estimate is hard to do since sizes of both vary).

I'd be wary to grate them, and if you can chop them up pretty small with a knife you'll probably be OK (especially if you use lots of onion, but it's hard to do unless it's a good knife).

Be extremely careful not to touch your eyes until you wash your hands really well after dealing with the onions. From experience, I can say this is quite unpleasant and I would urge you not to learn the same first-hand lesson, and it may sound odd that I need to mention it, but you'd be surprised how easily it happens when you're busy handling a decent number of onions that your hands are not adequately cleaned of the juice.

EGGS/FLOUR

The quantity of eggs and flour is a serious guessing game. Every time I make them I play around with it and see. There's no easy answer and no science.

The biggest key is the consistency of the batter and also the latkes as you are cooking them - go with your instinct.

If they're falling apart in the pan you may need more egg; but they can fall apart at the start when you first put them in and you can push it all back together in the pan.

But, if they fall apart when flipping then more egg and maybe flour (if too wet) is likely needed (though thickness and size will impact the fall-apart issue too).

I am making latkes tomorrow and so I looked at *Second Helpings* to see whether I needed to buy eggs. As I remember it, the recipe is 6 potatoes and 3 eggs, and for reference I believe it calls for 1 onion, which is ridiculously inadequate.

Bottom line - put in a bunch of egg and flour and see what it looks like - if it looks like your batter is just a lot of potatoes with a bit of stuff on it you probably need more of the stuff, but it should not look like soup.

Once you get to the point where you're cooking them, evaluate it as you go and adjust if needed.

You are certainly justified in tasting a latke (or two or three) early on for scientific purposes, to see if it's OK, and you should consider randomly testing quality at various intervals (almost certainly will be good, but you want to make sure, don't you?)

SO WHAT THE HELL IS THIS RECIPE???

As you will no doubt realise from these ridiculous emails, this recipe really is best written as unhelpfully as the following:

A bunch of potatoes

A bunch of onions

Some eggs

Some flour

Some salt and pepper

A generous quantity of oil (I use olive oil). (Quantities are flexible)

Trust your instincts.

COOKING TIPS

- Apron or clothes that can be ruined (all shirt layers, not just the top layer) - splattered hot oil will stain permanently;
- Consider oven mitts - small splatters are common and hands are the first to get hit;
- Stand back to the extent possible when putting in batter and be ready to jump if it splatters;
- Best safety tip is to not to make it too hot to start, and make it hotter as needed, but it has to be hot enough - you need a bit of a sizzle when you put in the batter, but not hot enough to cause a lot of splattering oil;
- Don't let the oil sit for too long in the pan before adding latkes (especially once you're rolling along) since it splatters more;
- Once you're rolling along (not the first batch) adding oil once latkes are in the pan causes less splattering BUT unless it's a really good pan you need some oil in there when you put in the latkes (you can lift each latke to let some oil under);
- You may need to add oil once you flip the latkes;
- Size/thickness is according to preference, but the heat needs to be relative - thicker means it can't be as hot or it will burn.

OTHER

Best to serve them immediately, while you are cooking. If not, you need some way to keep them hot (such as a covered dish, though that will usually soften the crisp out of them). This is one of the reasons why periodic pan poaching is recommended.

Consider running multiple frying pans, but don't get in over your head - I generally run 2 pans (sometimes 3) and I can handle that. The problem is not while cooking as much as at the transition stages when it get tricky because you don't want anything to burn, you don't want empty pans sitting on the burner too long or sitting too long with oil (gets really hot, can cause oil splatter) - you've got to remove them, put them on paper towels and continuously put down more paper towels, add oil and add batter all in a short time.

If someone is helping, you can use more pans and speed up the process and make the transition smoother. I recommend working together on the transition process with assigned roles, at least in the early stages, since otherwise you'll end up with a pan that's smoking hot and an ominous fear of what will happen when oil and latkes are added.

Consider putting the pan on a burner that's off if you find the transition is too slow.

Make sure there are large quantities of sour cream and applesauce available - don't go trying to go light or low sugar at this point, we're talking full out assault on virtually every diet ever conceived by human beings.

I think that covers it. Have fun with latkes and travels.

P.S. - have I mentioned occasional tasting?
Steven

To: Lauren; Joyce
From: Stephen
Subject: Latkes - a retrospective

I made latkes last night (it was planned, unlike my mother about 5 years ago, who, when I called to ask about latkes, decided to make them right then to provide me with the most authentic field-based information).

I used:
- 7 potatoes, mostly decently large and a few of them quite big (probably the equivalent of 10+ medium potatoes);

- 4 onions (2 medium and 2 small) but more would have been fine too;

- 8 eggs (I started with 5 eggs and discovered I was looking at potatoes with a bit of yellowy goop here and there; 3 eggs later it was looking right.);

- Probably about 1/2 cup of flour;

- A teaspoon or more of salt (undersalted if anything);

- 1/4 to 1/2 teaspoon of pepper;

- Note: when you squeeze/drain the potatoes don't worry about going crazy doing it - they'll ooze a lot in the bowl once the batter is mixed up (I forgot how much). If you make a little crater or two in the bowl the liquid will pool and you can easily scoop it out with a large spoon

From: Michael
To: Joyce; Steven
Cc: Donna
Subject: Latkes

Sometimes I wonder where I came from and then read email sagas like your latke instructions and think "I'm home!" Once in England I had written my mother to ask her the same question every modern Jewish child asks their parents when away. How do I make latkes? Moreover, how do I make latkes like you, because every year we go to some friend/cousin/ that serves the bad kind that get all soggy in the middle.

Given that she is a latkamatron she was able to take in inputs and outputs like an IBM mainframe.

D: "So how many people are you having over?"
M: "Ten."
D: "Ten?! You can't fit so many people in there! Where are they all going to sit?"
M: "I'm sure someone sat on a carpet somewhere in the Bible so I'll just say we sit on carpets."
D: "Carpets? That's not nice..."
M: "...ma, how many potatoes?"

I'm going to be in Mexico for the entirety of Hanukkah this year, so I'm either going to have to source good frying potatoes or innovate something from corn or beans. Globalization after all. Thanks for the (many) laughs.

Love,
Michael

An addendum:

Michael went to Mexico and decided to make homemade hummus except he couldn't find any tahini. So I got a call asking for help.

Did they have sesame seeds?

Yes.

As it was a long distance call for his friends, I told him I would take care of it and get right back to him.

I emailed a recipe to myself, copied and pasted it into a text message and within 5 minutes Michael had his recipe. He thought his mother was quite cool to do something like that and his hummus was a hit.

(I was kinda proud of myself for thinking of that too as a matter of fact).

Once we're on a food roll (and talking about Joyce), let me share a story about crêpes and whipped cream...

One weekend, when we were back in Montreal, Joyce called and invited us over for the evening. We were in the kitchen and Joyce decided we should make all the fixings for make-your-own crêpes. Once we were done with all the prep, she was going to call her brothers and their wives over and we'd all assemble our own crêpes.

So Joyce was busy making the crêpe batter and cutting up fruit. I was relegated to whipping the cream. Out came the

Mixmaster® and I started whipping the cream. As usual, the two of us were gabbing nonstop. I wasn't paying much attention to what I was doing and when I glanced away, the spatula got stuck in the beater blade and the whipped cream exploded everywhere!

It was on my hair, my clothes, my face and all over the window, the cupboards and the (oh yes) mini blinds that were over the windows.

Joyce started running like a chicken without a head to clean it up before it started hardening and turning gooey and I was trying to help (trying being the operative word). It's hard to concentrate, never mind see straight when you're laughing your head off.

I glanced upwards as something caught my eye. Outside on the balcony through the patio doors were cops in vests with guns.

I slid down against the kitchen island, holding my sides laughing and saying "What the hell, it was only whipped cream!"

Joyce came over as I was pointing towards the door and stopped dead. She opened the door to let the cops in.

All I could keep saying was "It was only whipped cream!".

It seems that as Joyce was cleaning under the kitchen cupboards, she pressed the panic button to the alarm and the police showed up.

Usually they charge an arm and a leg for a false call, but even though they refused some free crêpes, they also promised me they wouldn't charge her the fee. Instead they were going to milk the story for all it was worth and tell the guys back at the station that they found a redhead covered in whipped cream. Am I ever happy that I don't live in Montreal!

Speaking of Joyce and kitchens (this has nothing whatsoever to do with food...)

One day I was going over to Joyce and Michael's for a visit. As I left the house Dad said "Please ask Joyce what kind of perfume Auntie Charlotte likes. Her birthday is coming up and we'd like to buy her something".

Off I went.

What I usually did when they lived in their townhouse, was walk to their unit, and right next to the front door, where there was a full length window looking into the eating area of the kitchen, I'd press my nose against it and stay there until she turned around and saw me.

Joyce was always in the kitchen.

She saw me and let me in.

(Me)"Joyce, what kind of perfume does your mother like?".

"Why?" she asked.

I answered, "Because Mom and Dad want to get her something for her birthday".

"Why?" she asked again.

To which, (getting angrier by the minute) I answered, "I don't know, maybe because she's Mom's sister and they want to buy her something?"

"Why?" she asked yet again, now laughing her head off.

I got angrier. "What's with the why? Why can't you just answer my question?" I asked.

Through her laughter, Joyce answered, "I did. It's 'Y' by Yves St. Laurent®.

I almost killed her.

Bubby and Zaidy's dining room set:
Where memories come to life

5 IT'S ALL ABOUT FAMILY - MENTAL SNAPSHOTS

"Is your family bilingual?" A question I'm asked fairly regularly when people from other countries learn that I'm Canadian. What they don't expect is my answer, "Yes, we are. We're fluent in English and Pig Latin".

Dad spoke it often and taught us how to speak it when we were kids.

Mom's side of the family is unlike any other family I've ever known or heard of. I'm not saying that just because it's my family; I'm saying it because I believe it to be true. Mom's parents, Bubby and Zaidy were the most loving, warm, 'real' people you could ever meet. They didn't stand on ceremony. Family was everything to them.

When I was a toddler, Mom told me that one day she left me in the care of Dad in the back lawn. Dad did what Dads often do. He fell asleep. So I decided to go to my next favourite people — my grandparents. I crawled around the corner. I guess I knew not to go on the street (actually it's probably sheer luck that I stayed on the sidewalk) and wandered in my diaper. Evidently a man walking around the corner, picked me up, wet diaper and all, and went looking for my parents. Thankfully my mother claimed me or I could still be wandering to this day.

When I was very young, Bubby and Zaidy bought me a stuffed rabbit. It was one of those plush toys with a hard plastic face but I loved that thing. As an asthmatic, I didn't have dolls or stuffed animals in my room. I had the most sterile room on the face of the earth. Pink and sterile!

This bunny was precious to me. When I was about four and a half or five years old I had to have my tonsils and adenoids removed. I remember looking at Dr. Halpern as they were wheeling me to the operating room asking him why he was in his pajamas. The next thing I knew, I was awake with the sorest throat possible asking for my bunny and it was gone.

Mom had thrown it out.

I was devastated!

I still bug her about it. She told me it couldn't be washed anymore and it was time it went in the garbage. I never forgave her for that.

For years, as long as Bubby and Zaidy lived around the corner, I either got on my bike or walked around the corner to have a coffee (mostly milk) with Bubby before school. That was a precious time for me as I had her all to myself. She would make tiny birds out of candy wrappers, bunnies out of hankies and all sorts of other things. At the end of the day, Zaidy would be waiting for us to come home from school and had a treat of some kind. He was a fruit and vegetable importer and often brought unusual things, especially for that era.

I remember him bringing a coconut home for us to try. We had never seen one in real life. He took it out to the back patio and tried cracking it with hammer. That didn't work. Then he tried a hammer and screw driver. It took a while but he finally did it! He might have been the importer but Bubby was able to pick riper melons. Somehow she had the knack.

I used to go with Bubby to the fish store. Oh geez did it stink but I was enthralled with the huge live fish in a bathtub in the front of the fishmonger's shop. Once in a while one would jump out of the tub and have to be picked up and thrown back in.

Bubby would pick the best pieces of fish and make the most amazing baked carp or gefilte fish. She seemed to know the weight of it even before the fishmonger put it on the scale. She knew if it was too big or too small and always picked the perfect one.

I loved Friday night dinners at their house. The whole family (well those who lived in Montreal) went for dinner so I got to see my cousins and aunt and uncles. When I was younger, when Bubby and Zaidy lived around the corner in an upstairs duplex, Jeffrey and I would wait in small front room of the house and guess how many cars would go down the street before our fathers drove up from work. While we waited we took the bread board out of the kitchen counter into that small room, borrowed the huge bowl of filberts and walnuts from the table and played "nuts"; like marbles, except nuts we could eat while we were waiting for dinner.

When we tired of that we'd take out all the old photographs from the middle drawer of the secretary and share old memories. When I started high school they moved away closer to Auntie Charlotte and Uncle Saul. I was so upset but Bubby said "You had us for this long and now it's Charlotte's family's turn".

Bubby cooked for hours. She didn't have a food processor or dishwasher and everything was made from scratch. Friday night the array of dishes was mind boggling. Dad loved all the appetizers and had a field day with her chopped liver, meatballs or Halishkes. By the time the main course came along, he was too stuffed to eat any more. After dinner the women would congregate in the kitchen, put the leftovers away and wash and dry the dishes. It was a tradition and a time when we could just talk, catch up, share what was going on in our own homes and just have some special time with Bubby, Mom, my aunt and cousins.

Passover was special. By the time kids had kids and the family expanded, we had to move the Seder from Bubby and Zaidy's house to Auntie Charlotte and Uncle Saul's so they could extend the tables into the living room. I think we were around 40 people. Auntie Hadassah and Uncle Davey, Stephen, Howard, Dougie and Eric would come in from Newburgh, New York. I'd have my nose glued to the window pane on the side of the door, counting the minutes until they came.

They would stay a week which went by in a blink.

Jeffrey, Dougie and I would spend every waking moment together. We were all hockey fiends but nowhere near as much as Zaidy was. It didn't matter if we were in the middle of a Seder, he would whisper to Jeffrey or Kenny to run downstairs and check the scores. The holidays were always in the middle of the playoffs. He couldn't wait to finish dinner so they could run downstairs into the family room and watch the end of the game. That was in the days when there were fewer teams and hockey didn't continue to the end of Spring. Joyce was a riot. One Seder, Zaidy was impatient to finish the Seder so he could go and watch the rest of the game, Joyce turned to him and said, "Zaidy, you're going to sing every verse of every song" and wouldn't let him leave the table until we had.

I'll never forget going to a movie with my cousins Dougie and Jeffrey. Jeffrey was driving by then and had his own car. I think it was a Mustang. We got into the car and started driving to the theatre. It had rained a lot the day before so there were huge puddles. Jeffrey loved driving through them sending a spray of water everywhere. There was an older man in his 70s who saw him coming and vaulted over a hedge. Jeffrey wasn't going to soak him but it was hysterical watching this happen. There's many a memory of driving in a car with Jeffrey, but I'll leave that for another time.

Zaidy created the Ess Chai Family Club, named after his aunt Esther Chaia. I don't know of any other family who had a club, especially one which met monthly. At the beginning, the extended family would get together once a month at someone's home. Once it got too big they moved it to a synagogue on St. Urban. From there, they moved it to Victoria Avenue to an upstairs hall. The women would bake cookies and squares for the crowd. There were songs, skits and family report-outs. For the Purim and Hanukkah parties, all the young kids were invited. There was even a mock wedding which took place in the basement of our house.

Dad was the bride and wore Auntie Gilda's wedding gown. Our cousin Polly was the groom. And Uncle Saul was the pageboy. He rode around on my tricycle.

It was hysterical!

For more years than I can recall I think I spent a part of every weekend with my cousins Kenny, Joyce and Jeffrey at Auntie Charlotte and Uncle Saul's. Once in a while I'd sleep over and share a room with Joyce. She was my older cousin but went to bed so early, I'd sneak out of bed and go into the next room to watch late movies with Kenny.

Jeffrey and I did everything together; we were closest in age. Joyce was like my big sister and being the only two females in the immediate family circle brought us even closer. Kenny was my big cousin and the best hugger in the family. When things were tough, the first place I'd go was to Kenny's for one of his all healing hugs. And it always worked. I always felt better after one his bear hugs.

Years later, after Zaidy had passed away, and Bubby went into assisted care, we split up and had Friday night dinner at home and Auntie Charlotte and Uncle Saul's family did the same.

At that point, Bubby offered me their dining room set. It was more than a table and chairs; it was a place where a million memories were created. We sat around that table for holidays, and for Friday night dinners. We talked, laughed, shared what was happening in our day-to-day lives with each other. It was a gathering place more than just a surface to eat on. Her only request was that I take the plastic off the chairs. She had had the silk upholstered chairs covered with plastic because there were always young grandchildren and eventually great-grandchildren around making a mess. When I took the plastic off, the fabric was in perfect condition. Eventually I changed the covers to compliment our dining room colours, but rather than take off the old fabric, I kept it on and put fabric over it. It's still in perfect condition, safely tucked away beneath the new coverings.

Crocheted doilies are still in a drawer or two as is her crocheted table cloth that graced the table when it wasn't being used. One of her more intricate doilies is on the table now when it isn't being used. Even when the table became too small for the number of people we had, rather than sell it, we enlarged it to accommodate a larger crowd so new memories can be added to the old.

One summer I worked at Dad's factory Ansam in the Rosemount area, quite far from home. It was late on Friday and we were going to the car to drive home after a long week. Dad asked me to wait for him as he had something to tell Mickey, a man who worked for him, so I waited in the entrance to the parking garage.

And I waited and waited and waited.

No Dad.

Finally I went to look for his car and find him but the car was gone. He had left and forgotten me!

Off I went to get on a bus home. Thankfully I didn't have to transfer but it was a ride that took me from one end of the city to the other so a VERY long bus ride. I got home more than an hour late for dinner, walked into the kitchen and got an earful from Dad. "Why are you late? You know we have Friday night supper together!"

I looked at him, glared more like it, and answered angrily, "I'm late because you forgot me. I had to take a bus home. How many fathers forget their kids?!!" and stormed out of the kitchen.

All weekend he followed me begging, "Come on. Don't be angry. Talk to me." He'd point to his cheek and say "Give me a kiss. Don't be angry."

One thing I knew would get his goat; he used to hate when we turned on all the lights in the house. He'd run around closing them saying, "What do you think, we have shares in Hydro?"

So after this, I followed him around the house reopening all the lights. I was faster than he was. (Oh, and as we're from Quebec, we have unique ways of saying things. One is to open and close the lights, not turn them on and off. There are others but as I'm teased incessantly about that I'll keep the others to myself.)

Dad decided to make two new lines of clothes that year. He wanted to surprise me with one of them so left the newly designed tags on the foot of my bed so I should see them when I got home. I walked into my room and saw two tags, one called "Bananas. The line with appeal" (groan), and the other was the "Donna Mae" line. First of all, I hate my name and especially hate my middle name as I sound like Ellie Mae Clampett from the Beverley Hillbillies. Second of all, I don't spell my middle name with an 'e' on the end. It's May.

I walked into their room and asked "What are these exactly?" Dad answered, "Two new clothing lines. Do you like them? I wanted to surprise you." (I answered) "Dad, how do I spell my middle name?" to which he replied, "M-A-E?" I shook my head, and said, "You might want to have consulted with Mom before printing up all these tags. It's M-A-Y! like the month."

It took him a long time to live that one down.

As my cousin Michael R. says, in our family, when you're sick or need help, you don't get one person knocking at your door, you get a hundred. You might not want the hundred but they're there for you nevertheless. Our family are there for us no matter what.

One winter, Auntie Charlotte and Uncle Saul were in Florida and Jeffrey had broken his leg skiing. Mom was the point of contact so was called when he was brought to the hospital for x-rays. She went to pick Jeffrey up at the hospital in his cast with crutches. She brought him back to our house and I remember Zaidy hearing about it, getting on the phone with Jeffrey and saying "Now you're happy?" Jeffrey never sat still for any length of time, had more concussions from playing hockey than anyone I ever knew and, as far as Zaidy was concerned, this was the icing on the cake.

Once he was more comfortable with his crutches, I remember walking in and out of shoe stores in Snowdon with Jeffrey trying to talk the salesman into selling him one shoe. He didn't want to buy a pair as one would get worn and the other look brand new so figured, as they have one in the window, they could sell him just one. It didn't work. It was logical, but no one would do it.

As kids we loved going to Belmont Park with Mom and Dad. Dad was the biggest kid of us all. We would overdose on cotton candy and all the other stuff they sold at the Park but we would have the time of our lives! They had an huge wooden roller coaster right next to the water. I remember thinking that if one of the cars flew off the rails we'd be goners for more than one reason.

The best ride of all was the Wild Mouse. It was like a smaller roller coaster that had sharp turns. You'd sit 3 in a car, front to back, the car would shoot to the end, stop dead, make a right angle turn and would continue.

All we'd hear was "Oy, my kishkes". Poor Dad was at the back of the car and every time it would stop dead, two kids would slam into his stomach. We laughed more about his moaning and groaning than from the ride itself.

SNIPPETS OF MEMORIES

New York Skyline in the '60s

6 TRIPS TO NEW YORK

As far back as I can remember, we would go to New York City on the long weekend in May to shop for the year. After shopping in Manhattan we'd go to visit our cousins Ruthie and Lou, Jeffrey (or Jace as we call him) and Paul in Queens. On the way back we'd stop in Newburgh, New York to visit Auntie Hadassah and Uncle Davy, Stephen, Howard, Doug and Eric. Every visit was an adventure. In the city, we would shop 'til we dropped and had the fantastic meals. I was enthralled by the Automat.

It wasn't the greatest food, but it was an experience to eat there.

You'd put coins in a slot and choose the sandwiches, pieces of 'homemade' pie or cake and a beverage, open the little door and take out your food on china plates. As soon as you took something out, there was a woman in a uniform, small hat and all, behind the scenes to fill it with a fresh item. It was the precursor to vending machines but so much better, not to mention they had the best lemon meringue pie!

Every trip we'd take, we would go for one dinner to a favourite neighbourhood Italian restaurant called Mamma Leone's. It was a huge place and always packed and noisy but the food was fantastic. We couldn't wait to go back trip after trip and for the longest time, it didn't disappoint.

One evening we went to another Manhattan favourite called Danny's Hideaway. We often saw actors and actresses there before or after the theater. One night Marty Allen walked in. He was hard to miss with his wild and crazy hair. Shelly was mesmerized, especially as he came over to say hello. I didn't know where to look; at Marty Allen or Shelly who was so excited to meet him.

Our shopping expeditions were usually successful, except one trip where Dad bought Gerry a pair of Converse running shoes. He brought them to Camp Hiawatha where Gerry was going to play a basketball game. Gerry opened the box and there were two left shoes.

Did he return them?

No! Not Dad. He just bought two rights so Gerry ended up with two pairs of shoes.

When I was a young girl, we all went into Manhattan to shop and actually parked on the street which you could do in those days. When we went into the department store, the city was as busy as New York usually is but when we came out, there was a sea of people. It was packed and you could barely move. We walked over to the car to put our purchases in the trunk and watched as this cavalcade moved slowly down the street with a handsome man walking next to the car. He was the centre of attention. Like others nearby, we watched the commotion. People were walking with huge signs which had his picture on them and said, "Vote Kennedy for President".

He walked over to us to say hello and ask what brought us to New York, as we had Quebec license plates on the car. Mom and Dad spoke to him for a minute and then he knelt down and said to me "Do you know what it means to be President of the United States?"

I nodded, yes.

He took a button off his lapel, handed it to me and said "Well you hold on to this, because if I become President it might be worth a lot of money someday."

It was JFK.

I think Gerry was a little ticked off that he gave it to me and not him. I still have the button. It has a place of honour in my keepsake box on my dresser.

One trip Mom and Dad got tickets for all of us to see the Rockettes at Radio City Music Hall. We were really excited. Well, most of us were. Dad fell asleep in the middle of the matinee. Mom, Gerry and I were so embarrassed by the snoring that we got up and found other seats and left him there. He woke up trying to figure out where we'd disappeared to. We made like we didn't know him. On one trip, Mom and Dad thought Gerry and I were old enough to go to a show ourselves, so Mom dressed us to the nines, they took us across the street from our hotel to one of the Broadway theaters to see Fiddler on the Roof, and dropped us off. They were outside waiting for us when the show was over.

I felt so grown-up!

Our time with the New York contingency was always too short. Ruthie and Lou were a riot and we never knew what would come out of their mouths. Watching TV with Ruthie was an experience. She would scream and yell at the characters on TV as if they could hear her. I'll never forget watching the Wild Wild West show on TV when she started yelling, "Look behind you. He's going to hit you over the head!" We kept telling her, "They can't hear you!" but she still kept talking to them.

Time with Paul and Jace was precious. Every year we'd see them and it would be like time had stood still.

Ruthie taught me how to do needlework. We couldn't figure out why it was so hard for me to get it right until someone told her to sit opposite me instead of next to me. She was a leftie and I kept "screwing up the stitches" because they were backwards to hers. Sitting opposite her made he stitches work out right.

She got me hooked.

Their house was filled with needlework but she always seemed to find a spot for something new.

One trip to New York really stands out. That's when we drove to New York for cousin Howard's wedding. What an experience!

We drove with Jeffrey and Nessa. That was a car ride to remember. Jeffrey had a Camaro back then. The back seat wasn't very padded so every time he went over a bump we'd feel it BIG time.

How many bumps could one go over in New York City?

Many when it came to driving with Jeffrey!

The directions we got from Howard weren't the clearest.

"I think we need to be over on that freeway", Jeffrey said, as he drove across a field to get onto another freeway. And then, hearing "Nope, I think we have to be one over", looking at the next freeway in the distance.

Somehow he backed up onto an exit ramp to get us one highway over. We lived to talk about it and actually found our way to the hotel.

We went to check in and as Jeffrey and Nessa weren't engaged or married yet, and sharing a room was just not an acceptable thing in our family, Nessa and I shared a room. I didn't know her all that well, so it was an experience to say the least.

We had asked to have adjoining rooms so we could walk back and forth between the rooms especially when we were getting ready for the wedding. We got to the hotel only to hear that a blonde lady asked for us to be separated so they changed the rooms. Jeffrey and Gaby on the bottom floor on one end of the hotel and Nessa and I on the top floor on the other end. It couldn't be more separated if we tried!

We had them change it back. I gave my mother the cold shoulder the entire weekend only to find out it wasn't her; it was Auntie Charlotte!

During the day we went our separate ways to do some shopping. I went back to the room and there was Nessa walking back and forth on, not in front of, but on the dresser. Now why in the world would she be walking on a dresser one might wonder? Her answer, "I bought new shoes and the mirrors only go half way to the top of the dresser so I wanted to see what they looked like."

(My response) "Jeffrey, in case you don't know it yet, your girlfriend is wacko!"

She fit into the family perfectly!

Later that day we got ready to go to the out-of-towners dinner which was at a restaurant in the city. Again the instructions weren't that great. We found our way there but back was more of an issue for some reason. We were in one car with Jeffrey and Nessa, Auntie Charlotte and Uncle Saul took their own car with Bubby and Zaidy in the back and Kenny and Susan took their car, driving Joyce and Michael.

We were the third car in the caravan. We were stopped at a light. The light turned green and we watched Uncle Saul turn left, Kenny turn right and Jeffrey, being insistent that we should be going straight, went straight.

We got back to the hotel in a short period of time and then paced wondering what happened to the others. Kenny pulled in about 20 minutes later and then we all got increasingly nervous, pacing as we worried about what might have happened with Uncle Saul and gang. About 2 hours later they finally got back to the hotel. We were frantic by then. Kenny asked, "Where in the world did you go? We were so worried about you!" Being Uncle Saul, his answer was, "Who was in a rush?" Nothing phased him!

Before one of the family weddings in New York, we decided to leave a day early and go on a shopping expedition, en masse and descended on Cohoes first. I don't think the store ever recovered from our family invasion. Dad and Uncle Saul decided to sit on the landing and eat the egg salad sandwiches the staff plied them with, watching us run up and down, in and out of change rooms. The prices were exceptional so we were prepared to make a dent in our wallets. Every time I went to look for something, a sales lady would call through the store "Donna! Your cousin Joyce needs you in the dressing room!" Thanks to Joyce, I bought little as I didn't have time to look for any bargains.

We got back in the car and headed to nearby Albany. Next stop was Macy's. It was a huge two floor store with an escalator. We split up and started hitting the sales racks. I tried hiding from Joyce as (surprise, surprise), she wanted my opinion on everything she tried on.

I thought I was able to escape but nope, her husband Michael rode the escalator calling out "Donna! Where are you?" I think every sales person in the store singled me out. Finally I owned up to being Donna and went to find Joyce in the dressing room. So much for shopping. I saved a bundle that weekend!

Newburgh, New York

Every year on the way back from New York City, we'd stop in Newburgh, New York to visit Uncle Davey, Auntie Hadassah, Stephen, Howard, Dougie and Eric. As it was usually over the long weekend in May, and around Shelly's birthday, Auntie Hadassah always had a birthday cake for him. It was usually the only time, other than Passover, when we'd get to spend any quality time with them, although never enough time.

Uncle Davy was such an amazing man. He would ask us how things were going in school, not to make mindless conversation but because he really wanted to know. He listened to everything you would say. Education was extremely important to him, for his family and his community.

He loved music, especially opera. He learned Italian so he could understand what he was listening to. We had a connection around music as well. I loved symphonic music but hadn't developed a taste for opera. I loved listening to him talk about it, what his favourite operas were and how he used to love to go to his study downstairs, light a pipe and become immersed in listening to it.

For family milestones or events like a wedding or Bar Mitzvah we'd take that extra trip down to Newburg and we'd stay at the Hotel Newburgh which was kinda run down. Sometimes our extended family would take over the whole place and would run up and down the stairs from floor to floor, or in and out of the iffy elevator, willing it to get us to the floor we needed to be on. We'd be running in and out of cousins' rooms, checking wardrobes and planning what we'd do during the day.

Gerry and cousin Michael even got mugged on one of those trips, an experience to forget...

The rooms were ancient as was the old elevator. I think we took a collective breath whenever we'd walk into it but it seemed to always get us where we needed to go.

SNIPPETS OF MEMORIES

Maid of the Mist, Niagara Falls

7 NIAGARA FALLS

This story definitely needs a chapter of its own…

When I was 16 years old, I went with Mom and Dad to London, Ontario to our cousin's wedding. From there we went to Niagara Falls. On the way into town we stopped for lunch. It was a hokey, touristy place on the outskirts of town. There was a parking lot with a glass enclosure. Inside the enclosure were stairs taking you down a level to the side of a hill with a roof over it. There were souvenir shops, small snack bars and restaurants as well as kiosks where you could buy tickets for excursions.

We stopped for lunch.

Dad decided to buy a ticket for the next day to go on the Maid of the Mist under the Falls. He went to pay for lunch and to buy a ticket and we browsed through some of the souvenir shops. We lost sight of Dad so popped into every store to find him because it started to rain, and I mean pour; buckets-full, and we wanted to get to the hotel and check in.

We went upstairs to the enclosure hoping to find him there.

We always seem to lose him in shopping malls and excursions. This was no exception. He finally found us up the stairs. We thought he'd wait until the rain let up a bit but no, he didn't.

Angry at us for losing him, Dad ran to the car getting soaked. We thought he was going to pick us up. In the meantime the enclosure filled with other people waiting out the downpour.

We collectively watched Dad get drenched as he opened the trunk, take out an umbrella and bring it back without opening it.

"Dad, why didn't you just bring the car?" I asked, to which I received a very angry look back.

Dad handed me the umbrella, went back to the car getting even more drenched.

Everyone laughed.

Except Dad.

Actually there was steam coming out of his ears.

We drove back to the hotel and checked in.

We got settled in and decided to drive to the US side for dinner. In those days you didn't need a passport to cross the border so it was simple. Over dinner we made plans for the following day.

The next day we woke up and went to the restaurant for breakfast.

(Dad) "Donna, please hold onto my keys. I don't have pockets in my shorts."

So I put them into my purse.

The three of us wandered around the shops in the morning and then we left Dad so he could go to the Maid of the Mist and the falls, making plans to meet up back at the motel at the end of the day.

At 4:00 pm Mom and I make our way back to the hotel and stopped at the coffee shop for a coffee. The coffee came. I opened my purse to take out my sweetener. Instead I pulled out two sets of keys, one in each hand, looked at Mom and said, "Dad is going to kill me!"

Mom agreed.

We went back to the room, quietly opened the door and peeked in. Dad wasn't back yet. Of course not. He had to walk miles to get back to the hotel! About five minutes later, he walked through the door, looked at me and yelled, "I looked in every shop for you and couldn't find you. Do you know how far I had to walk to the falls?"

Telling him, "It serves you right. You shouldn't buy shorts without pockets," didn't exactly endear me to him. It just made him angrier. But when he started "Remind me to never travel with you again" yet again, that was it. I started laughing until my sides ached.

Mom joined in and the angrier Dad got, the more we laughed. He couldn't stay angry when he looked at the two of us hysterically laughing. He got that sheepish, smiling look on his face trying to hold back the laughter.

It didn't work.

I kept hearing the mantra, "Remind me to never travel with

you again" at least 10 more times on that trip and for many, many years to come.

8 ANOTHER CHANCE: OUR TRIP TO FLORIDA

Auntie Charlotte and Uncle Saul had a great condo in Aventura, Florida. They never used it in the summer months so encouraged Mom and Dad to use it. I was about 21 at the time. I had finished with my summer job and went with them to Florida for a break before going back to school.

This was towards the end of August when it was HOT! We drove to the condo, unloaded our stuff and Dad went to lower the temperature on the air conditioning to cool it off. It was really hot and stuffy in there.

We waited and waited and waited for it to kick in.

It didn't.

It just got hotter.

Auntie Charlotte had a list of phone numbers near the telephone in the kitchen. Dad called the repairman but it was late in the day and on a weekend, so his shop was closed.

Dad left a message on his answering machine to call us back, that we needed the air conditioner repaired.

We hadn't bought any groceries and it was getting hotter by the minute, so we decided to go for dinner and a movie for a bite to eat and to keep cool.

Back into the car we went and headed off to Pumpernicks Deli. They seated us very quickly. We watched waitresses running in all directions, keeping up with the demand. Finally, we gave our order to a seasoned waitress. She ran over to the counter to give in our orders and just as she walked over to the counter, the water main broke, gushing water like a fire hose right into her face.

Management told us to hang tight, that they would have it under control in a few minutes. Then the water rose and rose, above our ankles, continuing to pour into the restaurant.

At that point we were evacuated and went to find another place for dinner. After a quick meal we headed to the movie theater in a shopping centre nearby. We parked in the lot and as we wandered to the ticket kiosk, we passed a car with the windows shut in 95°+ degree weather with a Husky in the back seat, panting.

I ran to the kiosk, asked the ticket guy for help and then ran back to show him where the dog was. He jimmied the lock and opened a window, brought the dog some water and called the police.

Dog saved, we went into the theatre to see *The In-Laws* with Peter Falk and Alan Arkin. I don't think I ever saw my parents laugh so hard! Movie over, we braced ourselves to go back to the stifling hot condo.

If anything, even with all the windows opened, the condo was even hotter. I finally said to Dad "Let me fiddle with the controls and see what I can do".

(Dad) "I tried everything. It's one night. The repairman will come tomorrow and get it working, leave it alone."

I went to the controls anyway and saw he had turned off the air conditioning! I flipped on the switch and blissfully, cool air started streaming in.

It was my turn. "Dad; remind me to never travel with you again!" I had waited for years to say that!

This holiday was just beginning…

We got into a routine. We'd wake up, have breakfast in the condo, do something during the day like go to the flea market, wander in town, or whatever enticed us. Then in the afternoon we would go down to the pool and relax. Mom and I brought books and Dad 'took colour". Three minutes in the sun, and he would be black. For me one minute in the sun and I was the colour of a tomato.

I sat in the shade with Mom. Dad found a chaise to lie on, covered his eyes with those tiny plastic eyelid protectors and got all settled in to tan (and fall asleep of course). Mom and I became immersed in our books.

Dad talked.

We tried to read.

Dad talked, and talked, and talked. So Mom moved to another spot and I followed her. (Thinking back, that too was a trend).

Dad still talked. People would walk by and look at this strange man talking to no one. When he asked Mom a question and she didn't answer, he took off the eye protectors and (as he would say) felt like a 'yoyo'. We heard a lot about that.

However in the middle of hearing about his embarrassment and all the rest we were distracted.

There was a couple from New York who decided to go into the whirlpool. They were soaking and talking and enjoying the warmth.

The wife moved and started screaming "It had stripes! It had stripes! It's a brand new bathing suit!" and then looked at her husband and screamed "It was blue!"

We had no idea what they were talking about until they came out of the whirlpool and we saw the bottom half of their bathing suits had been bleached white. Someone had put too much chlorine into the whirlpool and the bottom half of their suits no longer had any colour. Laughing didn't exactly make them feel better. We couldn't help it. It was really funny looking!

When Dad got too hot lying in the sun he would perch on the ledge at the side of the pool. It was partially immersed so he could stay cooler and still be in the sun. Sun, lapping water = Dad falling asleep. Falling asleep meant snoring like a buzz saw.

So what does any normal daughter do in a case like that? Push her father into the pool. Every time he would start snoring, I would push him in.

It worked!

He'd stop snoring.

9 SNAPSHOTS OF MEMORIES FROM OTHER TRIPS

Other trips come to mind as I think back; one offs like Cape Cod and recurring trips for Michael's medical appointments and surgeries. There were the trips to Nassau, Bahamas and a last minute cancelled trip to Portugal because of a revolution which turned into a week away in Florida, just Mom and me, well until Dad decided he was going to come down and join us. There was my 16th birthday present trip from Grandma which was a trip to Zurich and Israel for a month, with Grandma, Mom and Dad.

Here are memorable moments for each of them....

Cape Cod

The five of us piled into the car and headed down to Cape Cod for a week-long vacation on the beach. Mom and Dad rented a small cabin which was really cool. It wasn't fancy or elaborate but had everything we needed. There was a tiny kitchen where we could have breakfast and some lunch and then we'd go out for dinner.

We got to Cape Cod, checked in to our small cottage near the beach, went to unload the car and then unpack. Dad went to change and realized he had no pants. He looked at Mom, upset because SHE forgot to pack his pants. As if that was her responsibility.

We all hopped back into the car and headed to a nearby shopping centre so Dad could buy some pants. As we walked back to the car, we saw a small airplane flying overhead, so close to the roof of our car that we hit the deck. We were sure the plane was going to hit the roof of the car. The runway was just across the street and the plane was coming in really low. Heart attacks adverted, we caught our collective breaths, got back in the car and headed back to the cabin. The week went by in a blur, from days on the beach to movies at the drive in theatre, it was a great trip overall.

Zurich and Israel

For my 16th birthday, my parents and grandmother asked me if I wanted a Sweet Sixteen party or a month away in Israel with a short stop in Zurich, Switzerland.

It was a no brainer.

I picked the latter.

We flew to Zurich first as Dad had business there. We stayed in this classically beautiful hotel on Lake Zurich called The Eden au Lac. I shared a room with Grandma. Mom and Dad were next door.

There were 2 high beds with beautiful linens, a small round table and two chairs in front of a balcony overlooking the lake. In the morning they would knock on the door of our room and bring a tray of freshly baked croissants, homemade preserves, churned butter and coffee with steamed milk, to start our day.

One morning, when we were having a more substantial breakfast in the hotel restaurant, Dad ordered imported cheese. We were talking and didn't think anything of it. A plate of cheeses came with the label *Canadian Kraft*. Dad looked at the waiter and said , "I wanted imported cheese, not cheese from home!" to which he replied, "Sir, I think you want domestic cheese, not imported."

There was that sheepish grin again.

The server took the Canadian Kraft away and brought some "imported cheese" from the region. That was something Dad wanted to forget, except it was filmed for all eternity.

Graham Kerr, The Galloping Gourmet was at the hotel restaurant filming one of his shows. When we got back to

Montreal, we turned the TV on and front and centre was the Galloping Gourmet from the Eden au Lac hotel in Zurich, and there we were! It's really too bad we didn't have PVRs back then or I would have taped it to tease Dad when he got home from work.

On Saturday evening they had a dinner cruise along the lake in Zurich which Dad bought tickets for. It was a great night until one of the locals walked over to ask me to dance. I didn't understand a word he said and wasn't too keen. Mom pushed me in his direction and off to dance I went. Some things just weren't worth arguing about with Mom.

A few days later we were off to Israel. We landed in Tel Aviv. It was a different world, nothing like I ever experienced.

We had a driver most of the time we were in there who took us to border towns and places we never would have gone to on our own.

One afternoon at the hotel in Tel Aviv, we were relaxing by the pool and waiters were running in and out of the bar bringing drinks to the people by the pool. One of the waiters had a terrible memory and would come over to us asking, "Did you order the Pina Colada"?

We'd say, "No".

He'd look around, shake his head, tell us he couldn't remember who did and would give it to us anyways. We had more free drinks that afternoon!

Walking through the lobby of the hotel to go back to my

room, I looked up and saw our neighbour from school who lived up the street. I went back to the pool only to hear Dad telling Mom and Grandma that he bumped into this guy's father. It was a small world.

Talking about a small world, a few days later we went to Jerusalem. We checked into the hotel and had arranged to meet our cousin Mark who had moved from Montreal to Israel and served a stint with the Israeli Army.

Grandma stayed in our room and was going to meet us downstairs a bit later. I left the room, slamming the door shut. They had just painted the hallways. The doors stuck and you had to pull them hard to close them. I heard a slam coming from the next room, turned to see who our neighbour was and came face to face with my great-aunt Leah.

It was her last day there on a tour. I told her to wait a minute, knocked on my door, and called out to Grandma, "Grandma, you have to come out for a minute. Your sister-in-law Leah is here and is staying in the next room."

She was in shock. None of us knew Auntie Leah had been travelling in Israel but it was great to see her. She was one of my favourites.

We explored the old city, went to the place where the Last Supper took place, went to the market to shop and just wandered.

There were conflicts back then but we didn't give it a thought. We went everywhere, through tiny winding walkways, exploring market stalls and alleyways. We went to the Wailing Wall, to synagogues, historic sites, and soaked in history I had only read about over the years. Here we were in the midst of it.

It was an extraordinary experience.

I remember most of it as if we were there just last month, not 45 years ago. We did everything from explore the Dead Sea area, watching Dad try to read a newspaper while floating upright in the salt-laden sea, to swimming at the gorgeous beaches of Netanya.

We had rented a condo there on, what Dad dubbed cardiac hill. We had to walk down (and then up) a cliff to get to the beach. But it was worth it as the beaches there were heavenly. I saw soldiers on breaks with their weapons on the beaches in Tel Aviv. Seeing them with their machine guns was really unsettling. We went to Haifa to the port and to the Baháʼí temple and hanging gardens, and to Yad Vashem which was the memorial to the holocaust. That place still haunts me.

We were driven to the Jordanian border. Our driver was armed in case there were any 'problems.' I loved some of the out of the way places which we wouldn't have known anything about if it weren't for our driver. The month went by in a blink but was the best gift I could ever had asked for; memories to last a lifetime.

Portugal With Mom, (well, almost)

The summer after my last year of high school, Mom and I decided we were going to go on a trip, just the two of us, so did some research and planned a week away in Portugal. Gerry and Karen had been there and loved it so that clinched it. Everything was set; flights, hotel, the works. I even went for a vaccination which was required. And then, a couple of days before we were to leave, there was a revolt. All travel was cancelled.

We still wanted to get away and didn't have much time to plan. Where does someone go when Portugal is out?

Florida. It wasn't our second or third choice, but it was a trip we could plan quickly without it costing a mortgage. Booking air travel a couple of days before a trip was even more ridiculously expensive back then. We booked a week in Hallandale. It wasn't as exotic, but we would still have time together. We booked the flights, the hotel, and about five minutes after everything was confirmed, the revolution in Portugal was over.

Since our tickets were non-refundable, Florida was in and Portugal out.

That's OK. We had a great time. We would go for walks in the evenings and then, on the way back to the hotel, stop to buy mini bottles of wine for the evening, sit on our balcony, have some wine and relax after a day at the beach or shopping or whatever we did.

Our week away, just the two of us didn't last long being just the two of us. Dad couldn't stand us being away for a whole week so showed up at the Hotel about 4 days in.

Graycliffe, Nassau, Bahamas

Mom and Dad knew this couple who managed a property in Nassau, right across the street from the Governor's Mansion. It was called Graycliffe.

There was the main manor house with an exquisite tiled pool and a separate pool house at one end. I stayed in the main house and Mom and Dad stayed in the pool house.

My room was enormous with a view of the pool and gardens. It was break time before midterm exams at school. I was so exhausted I remember falling asleep as soon as we got in the car at the airport and when I woke up, I panicked because they were driving on the wrong side of the road.

We got settled. I couldn't wait to get unpacked and down to the pool. We spent the day lounging and relaxing. I would bring my school work down and sit at one of the small tables by the pool to study. Even though there were umbrellas and a ton of shade from the greenery I fried and turned a bright shade of lobster. One of the maids from the main house took me to the front garden and cut down a leaf from a plant that was taller than I was. She squeezed out some gel from the leaf into a small cup and brought me back to my room to cover me with it. It was my first experience with aloe gel. It was right from the plant and helped my burn instantly. Within a day and a half it was almost gone.

We went helmet diving in the turquoise waters of the ocean. We would lower ourselves on the ladder at the side of the boat, and just as we were about to immerse ourselves, the guide would place heavy brass helmets over our heads which were attached to an oxygen supply. The front was of glass so we could see the marine life around us. The helmets were very heavy but being submersed made a difference as the water made them more buoyant. Once we hit the bottom, our guide would make hand motions and then the magic happened. He had trained fish in their natural habitat who did all sorts of tricks for us. It was mesmerizing.

Unfortunately we had to cut our trip short. Bubby and Zaidy were in Florida at the time and Zaidy had a heart attack. We went back to Montreal with Dad and Mom went to Florida and stayed with Bubby to help with Zaidy and make sure he was well cared for.

Norfolk, Virginia

Michael's surgeon moved from Montreal to Norfolk, so we had to follow her. We would take trips yearly; pre-op, post-op, and for surgeries. Every year that Michael would be operated on, Mom and Dad would get in the car and drive down to Norfolk. They were our rock.

When Michael was really small, he had left his doggy pillow in Syracuse, New York, in the hotel room where we stayed over on the way down to Norfolk. He was devastated. Mom and Dad took a detour to pick it up and safely delivered it to Michael.

They were adopted by the community as much as we were.

People would invite Mom and Dad into their homes for Shabbat dinner. Someone had donated tickets to the baseball game to Ronald McDonald House. Miss Ellie, the manager didn't know what to do with them because the families who were there were over at the hospital with their kids.

Mom and Dad didn't want to go, but instead of letting the tickets go to waste, he took them all and went to the ball park to sell them and bring whatever money he got back to Ronald McDonald House for a donation. He almost got arrested for scalping but talked his way out of it once the police knew where the money was going.

Norfolk become our home away from home, way too many times to count, but the family came with us.

Mom and Dad would stay with Michael so I could get an hour's sleep here and there or go to the cafeteria for a bite to eat. They sat with me in the surgical waiting room for hours on end doing puzzles and just being there so I would have the support I needed.

That's what our family is all about.

Camp Hiawatha Waterfront

10 CAMP HIAWATHA

Every summer from the time I was 7 years old, I'd go to Camp Hiawatha for 8 weeks of sleep-away camp. Some people would wonder how in the world my parents could send me at such a young age but it was a family tradition. Dad went to the same camp when he was a kid and the three of us followed.

At least a month before camp, we'd hit the Camp Shop where we'd buy everything from camp blankets to duffle bags, to new Hiawatha white and green T-shirts. Mom would sit for hours at a time sewing on name tapes on every item of clothing, on socks, sheets, you name it. She had to do that for three kids which was no easy feat.

There was a separate boys and girls camp on opposite sides of the lake. You could go from one to the other via the road to the camp or along the water on a path that hugged the lake shore. To be able to go boating and water skiing, you had to pass your swim test which meant you had to swim from girls to boys camp or vice versa.

Gerry and Shelly went to Hiawatha as did Jeffrey and Kenny. Joyce refused. We tried to change her mind but to no avail. I really wanted her to go as she was like my sister. We have a male-dominated family so pretty much everyone else was in boys camp.

Mom and Dad used to visit us all the time as the country house was close by and it was a 20 minute car ride to camp. After a few years, Bea and Bernie, the owners, asked them not to come as other kids whose parents didn't live close by weren't coming and kids were getting homesick.

Even so, because Dad was an alumni, we got to see him within the first 2 weeks of camp. There was a tradition, the counselors would play the campers in a Braves baseball game. Dad would come to be the coach so I'd get to see him as I watched Gerry play in the game. Actually, he'd come up every Saturday to coach the baseball games so would have an excuse to be there and we'd get to see him.

Kenny worked with Bernie so would be in girls camp quite often. When I saw the old white Cadillac parked at the office, I knew Kenny would be around and it would make my day!

For movie night, Kenny would sit in a chair operating the projector and I got to sit with my big cousin as he ran the movie. As I was asthmatic, almost every year, at least when I was small, Dad would visit me, and if I didn't have a suntan, he would declare that I must be sick and would take me back into the city to see the doctor.

More times than I'd like to admit, he was right. Doctor's orders were that I had to be in an air conditioned environment.

That sucked. I bugged them constantly to let me go back. Most summers I did, although usually ended up sleeping in the infirmary. I had my own room in there, but even so, I still insisted on going back to camp. The camp mother figure, Aunt Aidy lived in the infirmary and was in the next room to me. When I'd have a rough night she'd come into my room and scratch my back to calm me down and help slow my breathing. Whenever she'd call Mom and Dad, they knew it was time to come and pick me up and take me back into the city to see Dr. Bacall.

We had the greatest cook at Hiawatha. He was a chef from Ruby Foos and would quit every summer so he could take the job at camp. On Friday evenings we had kosher style Chinese food. That was the best part of Friday night. Once in a while, during Colour War or for Visiting Day, he would set up grills that would span the side of the baseball diamond and make Harry's famous BBQ chicken.

We never suffered for great food at that camp. Funny enough, when Michael was old enough to go to camp, Hiawatha wasn't around anymore so he went to Pripsteins. When we went to visit him on Visiting Day, he told us about their cook and the amazing BBQ chicken he made. I told him that Harry the Cook made the best chicken in the world so this had to be the second best chicken.

Michael said "Our cook is Harry too!" I was dumbfounded. I didn't think Harry was still alive never mind cooking. He cooked at Pripsteins until he died. He must have been in his 80s.

But I digress...

For Colour War, I couldn't participate as my breathing wouldn't allow it, so they created a special role just for me. I was part of the Quarter Master Corps. There were judges for the 3 days. I helped the judges keep track of the scores, and monitor some of the events. It was great to take part even though I didn't take part if you know what I mean. I remember one tug of war when Shelly pulled the rope so hard he broke his elbow. That was not pretty.

On Visiting Day we had to wear Hiawatha White and Green colours. That's when the parents brought boxes of candy and cookies, homemade favourites and other toiletries and things the kids needed.

When I was younger, we'd keep our stash and eat it whenever we wanted. Unfortunately some of the kids' parents didn't show up or sent surrogates for Visiting Day and the kids got little or nothing in the way of goodies, so we decided to let the kids keep one of two of their absolute favourites. The rest we would pool into a huge box or laundry basket and every day the kids could pick a couple of things out of the community junk food box. That evened things out a bit.

Twice a week there would be canteen where you could choose a pack of candy or chocolate bar and a drink and some toiletry items if you needed, like toothpaste etc. and it would go on your camp bill for the parents to pay at the end of the summer. There was no shortage of sugar that's for sure!

We had socials every Thursday night when boys and girls camp got together in the huge social hall on the boys camp side. We put on a play every summer and did a great job with sets, music and some great acting. I loved helping them paint the sets for the plays and remember most of the songs from Oliver and the Music Man even to this day.

Brian B. was a great play director, played the piano and taught us all the songs. I can still see him in my mind's eye sitting down at the upright piano in the social hall playing everything from Gershwin to Broadway hits. He was amazing!

We weren't allowed to have any electrical appliances in our bunks so when we'd wash our hair, we'd have to take our hair dryers to the social hall, sit on wooden benches around the periphery of the hall and dry our hair. When it was storming, we'd take our shampoo outside and wash our hair in the rain. Some summers the weather was so cold and rainy we'd end up in our bunks for days on end.

We'd play jacks and card games, read, draw, or just drive each other crazy. We also did raids on some of the other bunks, nothing too horrible but enough to get us into trouble.

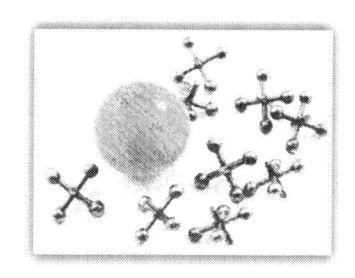

I remember one of the raids when we were seniors and hooked up microphones in the girl's washroom during one of the socials. The girls would congregate in there and talk about which guys they found the cutest or who was going after whom. It was broadcast right across the camp. We would 'French' the sheets on the bed, where we'd fold the bottom sheet over in half and fold it over the blanket so when someone would get into bed, their feet would rip a hole right through the sheet.

The Seniors at camp would be allowed to go into town for an evening here and there. We'd be bused into Ste. Agathe and we'd go to a movie and then out for pizza to Tevere's or to Laurentian Bar for a bite. Before curfew, we'd take taxis back or grab a lift with one of the counselors.

When I was older, I went back as a counselor every year until I was 19. Every day before the kids would go to sleep, the councilors would go into the dining hall where loaves of white sliced bread would be on the tables along with a huge, white, plastic bucket of peanut butter and another of strawberry jam and we'd make 'mongs' for all the kids.

I have no idea why they were called mongs. We'd take orders beforehand as some wanted only peanut butter, some only jam. We would make a pile of sandwiches for the kids to eat just before bed and bring them back to the bunks. Looking back I'd say that was probably one of the worst nutritional things we could do but the kids wolfed them down and then went to sleep. I don't remember any of the kids ever being allergic to peanut butter like so many are today...

I'd see the family on my days off when I'd go to our country house but on the way back the tradition was that we'd stop in Ste. Agathe, go to Laurentian Bar or stop at the small corner store at the cutoff to Ste. Donat to pick up Charm lollipops for the kids or some other coveted treat.

After the summer was over and the kids packed up and left camp, we, as counselors would meet up with them about a week or so later at the Orange Julep. That was our unofficial camp reunion location.

Even at the Shiva for Dad, some of our fellow campers and counselors came to pay their respects. For some reason, they all came on the same day just by chance and we reminisced and shared the memories we loved best. You can take the Frieds out of camp but you can never take camp out of the Frieds.

DONNA KARLIN

11 MOVING AWAY & TRIPS BACK HOME

In 1976 I got married and moved away to Ottawa. It was supposed to be for one year and then we'd move back. Instead we ended up staying. It was hard for me as I had such close ties with the family. Who knew there would be a referendum with a threat by Quebec wanting to secede from the country? There was no point in going back to Montreal. Instead, we found jobs we loved and stayed in Ottawa.

We went back 'home' every weekend as we subsidized my income by playing in my father-in-law's band for weddings and Bar Mitzvahs. As most of the gigs we played were for Jewish events, they were often on Sunday evenings which meant driving back to Ottawa either at 2:00 am or 5:30 the next morning. It was brutal as I was working 7 days a week.

Once I got a job with the Symphony I quit the weekend gigs which meant actually making a life in Ottawa. It was a great place to live, low key and beautiful. It was close enough to

Montreal where we could go back even for a day if we wanted. Every weekend we could, we'd drive straight to the country as long as the house was there and relax before diving back into the week ahead.

Once Michael was born and we were seeing a surgeon in Montreal, we would go back even more regularly. I had given up my job with the orchestra to work with Michael. We would sometimes stay for days at a time for Michael to have medical tests. Mom and Dad bought a crib and put it in my old bedroom. They had already moved Gerry's furniture in there, so there were two couches that became beds if needed.

After Michael's first surgery I pretty much moved back into my old bedroom on Dufferin Road. We were there on and off for almost 3 months and for his post-op visits until he was about two, before his surgeon moved to Norfolk, Virginia. Here was another generation, and my son, back in my old room. We were coming full circle.

Just as I had many 'firsts' in that house; first steps, first words, first everything pretty much, Michael had some firsts there as well in the same kitchen on Dufferin Road, playing with the same Tupperware®, zooming around the kitchen in his walker and even eating his first bagel. What was really special for me, was watching him take after me when it came to exploring that room. He would sit on the floor, open the cupboards and see how much of a mess he could make. Thankfully it wasn't with shoe polish and detergent; Mom had moved those years before into the laundry room.

One of his favourite cupboards was in the peninsula where Mom kept the extra grocery bags. He would take them out one by one and throw them up in the air, watching them float to the floor with such a look of glee on his face, it was priceless.

The family surrounded us, visited us daily and made sure I had everything I needed on an emotional level. Joyce and Michael L. would come and wake my Michael up. Michael L.

wouldn't take no for an answer even if Michael was fast asleep. He would walk quietly into the room and wake him up and the two would whisper to each other all kinds of things. For some reason my Michael would call Michael L. 'Tuna Fish'. I can't remember why but I do remember when Michael found out that Michael L. had a brother, he asked if he was called "Salmon". Joyce and Michael were Michael's god parents. Joyce used to call him her "Godboy".

Dad worked with Sport Maska, CCM / Starter and because of that, Michael had an official Montreal Expos hat and jersey when he was a toddler and a Montreal Canadiens official jersey when he was a year old. Dad hung out at the Montreal Forum a lot. He was like a kid in a candy store. Who wouldn't want to hang out with the team? When Michael was in the Children's Hospital in Montreal, after his first surgery, some of the players would check in on Sam's grandson to make sure all was well.

On some weekends, when Michael was a bit older, we'd go to the Forum with Dad to watch the players practice. Michael had a sticker book which you would get in the grocery store. The book was free. The sticker packages you bought to fill the book with was what cost because you had to keep buying the packets until the whole book was filled. That was for one year. The players and the book changed from year to year.

One particular visit to the Forum, Michael brought his sticker book with him to show the players and so he could get their autographs.

He had a dilemma. Some of the players found their names and signed the book in the square where their sticker was supposed to go. Michael got really upset and started to cry.

Larry Robinson asked him what was wrong. Michael told him, "What am I going to do when I get the sticker now? I have nowhere to put it!" to which some of the players responded, "Don't worry, Michael. The autograph will be worth a lot more than the sticker. Just put the sticker somewhere in the margin but keep the signature.

Some of the players would pick him up and skate around the ice with him. I don't know who was more excited, Michael or me and Dad just sat there with an ear to ear grin on his face. He was in his element.

When Dad turned 50, I made a special cake for him, a reproduction of the Montréal Canadiens jersey, crest and all. We drove into Montreal with this huge sheet cake on my lap the whole way. Every Maislin truck driver we passed honked their horn when they looked down and saw the cake on my lap. I figured Dad would bring it to the Forum and eat it with the players.

Nope.

He refused to cut it.

It sat in the pan for about a month before it turned to cement and we had to throw out the cake and pan when he left the house. Was he ever angry! But we had to throw it out before it got moldy and turned green.

Moving away was one of the hardest things I ever did but not moving back was probably the hardest, at least when it came to family. I missed seeing many of the next generation go to school and grow up. I miss not being able to have the family dinners around Bubby and Zaidy's table and continue some of the traditions that were started generations ago. I miss stopping in to see Joyce and putter around the kitchen with her, I miss the conversations that I used to have with Gerry or finding time to take Shelly for a bite and to catch up.

I know all of the family's successes and milestones, but I'm too far away to celebrate them all in person on a moment's notice. I don't have the same mental snapshots I had way back when and living in another city, even though close enough even for a day's drive, creates a separation. I would love to celebrate my successes with them as well.

I talk with Mom at least once a day but it's not the same as popping into the apartment and sharing life situations and whatever we happen to want to talk about. I'm lucky that I live in a great, family-oriented city and have made a ton of friends here and in the many parts of the world where I work. Still, it's not the same as being able to get in the car and pop over to see Mom, my brothers, Auntie Charlotte or my cousins. So I store the memories of the snippets of time I have with them in the back of my mind and to be able to recall them when I'm missing them so much.

When I'm back in Montreal, I memorize the warmth of being back in my home town, so I can recall it in my mind's eye, I want more face-to-face conversations with all their details and depth, to share the day to day ordinary life my family members are living.

That's how I keep them near even from far away.

12 SOME MORE RANDOM SNIPPETS

Zaidy used to sing all sorts of songs; two of the most memorable were "It's a Long Way to Tipperary" and the other was "I've Got a Lovely Pair of Pants". I've heard the first one in movies and such but the second song? I have no idea where it came from. As Zaidy grew up in Liverpool, England, I'm thinking it's an English thing.

Any of you who knew him will remember this song with an inner smile, as he sang it all the time.

I've got a lovely pair of pants
Talk about the fashion that you get from France
You can never match them,
I've had to patch them.
I put them on last Sunday night
I did I do declare.
Everybody smiled but I got wild
When they all began to stare----

At my naught naught naughty little patch behind
At my naught naught naughty little patch behind.
I turned round, and cried "Oh Lord!"
What does the whole gang want around me for?
But one sweet girl with her hair in curls
To me she was most unkind
For she cried, "Oh Jack,
I'd love to have a smack at your naughty little patch behind."

I had a pain the other day
Hastening to the doctor living down our way.
I asked him to cure it.
I could not endure it.
He said to me, "You're very very queer
And you ought to be in bed,
Now answer very plain. Where is that pain?"
So I turned to him and said,
"In my naught naught naughty little patch behind,
In my naught naught naughty little patch behind."
"Take my advice, and put a little ice
On your naughty little patch behind."

Dad was very superstitious. We had to be careful of so many things it was hard to count.

(Dad) "Don't put your hat on the bed."

(Me) "Why not?"

(Dad) "I'm not sure what the reason behind it is, but it's bad luck."

SNIPPETS OF MEMORIES

(Dad as someone would go to pass him a scissors or a knife) "Put it down first."

(Me) "Why?"

(Dad) "Because it's bad luck."

(Me) "Why, Dad?"

(Dad) "I don't know the reason behind it. It just is."

(Me) "Dad, it's a good thing you're not a surgeon. Scalpel. "Put it down first". Dad groaned. I shook my head. We all put a sharp object down before we gave it to him.

Once I came into the house. It had been pouring so my umbrella was soaking wet. I went to open it to let it dry in the foyer.

(Dad) "Never open an umbrella inside."

(Me) "Why not?"

(Dad) "It's bad luck."

(Me) "In what way is an open umbrella bad luck?"

(Dad) "Do you have to question everything I say?"

(Me) "When it's about an open umbrella, yes I do".

(Dad) "Just don't do it."

If we bought a new purse or wallet, he would have to give us money to put in it. If someone moved into a new apartment or house, we had to give them a broom, box of salt and a loaf of bread to chase away all the bad spirits and to make sure they always had what they needed.

That is one superstition that is more like a tradition and makes some sense. I'm still not sure about the hat or umbrella.

If a black cat crossed the street, we didn't go until someone else had broken its path. That was a given in our family. Dad missed an entire fishing trip because of that when he was younger. Who else was driving in the back roads of the country at 4:30 in the morning? I think Grandpa disowned him for that one.

We never walked under a ladder, made sure we tossed salt over our shoulder if any was spilled and constantly questioned him as to why.

We never did get a good answer.

IN SUMMARY

What is family? Families are made in the heart. They're the ones who bear witness to my life. They're the ones who accept me for good or for bad. They show up and are there regardless of what's going on. They might get angry with me but through the anger, I know there's immeasurable love. Too often they become so wrapped up in their own lives that they forget their family is there, but when push comes to shove, they reappear. And when we need them, they're there in a heartbeat.

Sara Dessen, in her book Lock and Key, describes what family is so perfectly when she says, *"What is family? They're the people who claimed you. In good, in bad, in parts or in whole, they were the ones who showed up, who stayed in there, regardless. It wasn't just about blood relations or shared chromosomes, but something wider, bigger.*

We had many families over time. Our family of origin, the family we created, and the groups you moved through while all of this was happening: friends, lovers, sometimes even strangers. None of them perfect, and we couldn't expect them to be. You can't make any one person your world. The trick was to take what each could give you and build your world from it."

Our family isn't perfect by a long shot, but to me, for me, they are.

Mom and Dad taught me everything they could so I could build a life around the learning. Mom told me years ago that she brought me up to be strong and independent.

That she did.

She taught me to stand on my own two feet, to deal with whatever came my way and I could because I always knew my parents were there for me.

New tales are continuously interwoven with old memories; each new generation strengthens our family bonds and creates memories of their own.

Dad would call and say "I'm in the neighbourhood. I want to drop in for coffee". His idea of 'neighbourhood' was seeing a customer in the outskirts of Montreal, two hours from Ottawa. He would have a hankering to see Michael and drive all the way to be here for when he got home from school, have a coffee and get his 'Michael fix' and then turn around and go home. He drove to Ottawa like most people stopped in at the grocery store.

I sometimes had to separate them in restaurants and cars, but watching those two together, was priceless. The love is evident in Michael's tribute to his grandfather at his funeral and subsequently his Facebook page where he said:

"When I was seven years old, I once said to my Zaidy Sam: "If you would only behave, we would be the best of friends." This turned out to be a weak ultimatum, because we were the best of friends and he rarely behaved.

Around me, he was a jovial clown with a deep belly laugh that could coax a smile out of anyone, even in less-than-appropriate situations. But I had only seen the silliest sliver of a complex man.

When I was a boy, I never knew the man who was the life of the legendary Lac Paquin parties. The man that consorted with big shots at the clubs and cabarets that dotted Montreal when it was an icon of the world in the 1950s.

To a boy, he was the consummate storyteller. He would take me for drives through winding streets where abandoned factories once sewed the world's fashions, and painted stories with such enthusiasm and detail that I would swear that there were ghosts standing outside of those old brick buildings. The stories sometime came true.

When I was nine he introduced me to Bob Gainey and the entire 1989 Montreal Canadiens, who almost won the Cup that year. Between the two of us, I wasn't sure who was more excited, despite him having met these guys a hundred times before.

I never knew him in business either. There are more appropriate people to tell those stories. What I know is that he loved the art of making a deal more than the deal itself. He would describe sales like one would describe dancing. He told me of exotic trips to Europe or China, meeting fascinating people to score the big deals.

He never lost that love of the kibbitz; just two months ago he would score his last, and told me about it with such pride. He still had his game. But I didn't know that to get there, he had to overcome obstacles, doubts, expectations. He found his own way in life, reinvented himself, refused to be defeated by events. He was fiercely loyal to his family, and when they were in trouble, set aside the clown for a bright and intense desire to do right by them.

To me, that was most evident when I was lying in a hospital bed, hurting. All of that history and complexity cleared away to reveal a man with nothing but love to give. He drove 2,200 km to fetch my favourite stuffed animal that I forgot and brought it to my room at the Ronald McDonald House in Norfolk, Virginia.

He called every day to check up on his "little man."

Over the years, his layers were revealed to me as my perception matured. I have tried to retrace his steps despite this city shifting so quickly under changing times. As I grew older, I realized that the places and people were larger than life, animated versions of their real selves.

At first, I was amused, thinking "Oh Zaidy, there you are

being like a big kid again." But as I entered my 30s, I began to see the lessons hidden in the tales he would tell, and they imprinted themselves onto me:

- *That the honourable path is more difficult than the easy one, but also the more just,*
- *That there is a piece of your childlike self that lives deep inside you, and you should never, ever let it go,*
- *That you should never stop telling your wife how beautiful she is, even if it's a hundred times a day,*
- *And that no matter what life throws at you, you never forget to laugh.*

When he was a boy, my Zaidy would watch men like Camillien Houde parade down the city streets, chatting up friends and strangers in top hat and tails, always with a firm handshake for the men and wink for the ladies.

Montreal was a boomtown then, a centre of the world, when money stuffed the pockets of those with the chutzpah to grab opportunity. Zaidy, his beautiful Pauline, family, friends and acquaintances wrote a piece of Montreal's mythology. He was emblematic of the shmata racket, importers and jewelry sales. He threw big parties and gave big tzedakah and loved every joke told to him. Like the city, he suffered a decline in luck once or twice, but never for a minute lost his joie de vivre. He never let language politics or religion get in the way of friendship. He fed on a steady diet of hot dogs, les Habs, dancing and kibitzing. Like the city, he kept one arm around tradition and another around the new. He was born in, and died in, the city that he had become an inextricable part of.

When I was 11 or 12, my Zaidy told me that he was friends with Jean Béliveau. Even then I thought it was a tall tale. He grinned and winked at me, like he was insinuating that I caught on to one of his little ruses.

Only for my birthday, I received a #4 Canadiens sweater and hat both signed and addressed to me. I have them both to this day.

Fitting in a way that they should pass so close to each other.

Jersey when Michael was an infant and Jean Beliveau jersey & hat

While a small piece of Montreal has died today, he leaves a legacy of love, of honour, and of panache. The man who looked up to big shots became one, at least to me and my family.

Wherever he is now, he'll be the life of the party.

After Jean Béliveau passed away, Michael joked that Dad was probably driving him crazy 'up there' and that Jean Béliveau would be too polite to do anything about it. I think he's right!

Life goes on. It's different without Dad, many would say a lot quieter, but it does go on. And Mom, well, as she has my entire life, she continues to blow me away with who she is, all she does and how much insight and energy she has.

This book isn't words of wisdom or lessons to learn. Rather it's how I grew up and all the love, insights and humour I was surrounded with. I am blessed with a huge extended family. Cousins are like brothers and sisters, not distant relatives. When we get together time seems to stand still.

And there isn't a day that goes by when I don't think of them in some way, or recall a memory so vivid that it seems to come to life all over again. So Joyce, when I hear Calendar Girl sung by Neil Sedaka, I remember the two of us singing it at the top of our lungs in Mom's kitchen. Kenny, when anyone says "hugs" to close an email, all I think of is you and your amazing, healing, loving hugs. And Jeffrey, there are so many memories that we share, I can't even begin to tell you how many times in a day you come to mind.

Thankfully with Facebook and the Internet, we're able to stay in touch with family wherever they are. Still, I wish we were all gathered around Bubby and Zaidy's table, sharing what's happened in our lives of late amid tons of laughter. And I hope together we create many more wonderful memories in the making for a long time to come.

ABOUT THE AUTHOR

Donna started off as a professional percussionist in a world class orchestra. Life circumstances guided her in a different direction and she became a Coaching Psychologist.

To Donna, work is play. She is an author, keynote speaker, and lecturer and is internationally recognized as a pioneer in the field of leadership coaching. She's been called a pot-stirrer, thought shifter and reality checker and is best known as The Shadow Coach®.

For 32+ years, Donna has worked with global leaders to develop the competencies and practices that enable them to meet the challenges of the future. She brings a dynamic, strengths-focused perspective to executive leadership development.

Principal and founder of A Better Perspective® and The School of Shadow Coaching®, Donna works on five continents with Heads of State, Ambassadors, High Commissioners, leaders in the Military and Security and Intelligence realms, Task Forces, C-Suite leaders, medical professionals and innovators who are impacting social transformation and inclusion around the world. Donna is a SupporTED Coach, a member of the team that coaches the TED Fellows, and Coach at The Unreasonable Institute.

She is on the Advisory Council of The International Academy of Behavioral Medicine, Counseling and Psychotherapy (IABMCP), communications advisory and head of the Advisory Board for INSPIRIT International Communications, Brussels, Belgium, and a Founding Fellow of the Institute of Coaching Professional Association, Harvard Medical School.

Her work has been written up in Fast Company Magazine, The National Post (Financial Post), The Globe and Mail, The New York Times Business Section, The Boston Globe, and Personal Success Magazine. She has authored the critically acclaimed, award-winning book, *Leaders: Their Stories, Their Words - Conversations with Human-Based Leaders*, and *The Power of Coaching: Don't Give up Your Day Job, or Should You?*

She is a Master Corporate Executive Coach, she was awarded a Postgraduate Certification in Executive Coaching, she is certified in Organizational Psychology with focus in Executive Coaching by The Professional School of Psychology and Certified as a Diplomate in Professional Coaching by the IABMCP.

Donna "defected" from Montreal (according to her family who still hasn't gotten over it) and, for the past 39+ years has been based in Ottawa, Canada.

If you ever wondered why Donna is the way she is, this book will definitely put things in perspective.